WHEN
BAD THINGS
HAPPEN
TO
GOOD PEOPLE

Harold S. Kushner

WHEN BAD THINGS HAPPEN TO GOOD PEOPLE

Schocken Books · *New York*

First published by Schocken Books 1981
10 9 8 7 6 5 4 3 2 1   81 82 83 84 85
Copyright © 1981 by Harold S. Kushner

Library of Congress Cataloging in Publication Data
Kushner, Harold S.
When bad things happen to good people.
1. Theodicy. 2. Kushner, Harold S. I. Title.
BM645.P7K87   296.3'112   81–40411
                        AACR2

Manufactured in the United States of America
Designed by Nancy Dale Muldoon
ISBN 0–8052–3773–9

The author makes grateful acknowledgement to the following:

The Free Press, a Division of Macmillan Publishing Co., Inc. for permission to quote
from FAITH AND DOUBT OF HOLOCAUST SURVIVORS by Reeve Robert
Brenner, 1980, Copyright © 1980 by Reeve Robert Brenner.
Fortress Press for permission to quote from SUFFERING by Dorothee Soelle, 1975,
Copyright © 1975 by Fortress Press.
Harcourt Brace Jovanovich, Inc. for permission to quote from ANATOMY OF
FAITH by Milton Steinberg.
Media Judaica for permission to quote from LIKRAT SHABBAT compiled and
translated by Rabbi Sidney Greenberg and edited by Rabbi Jonathan D. Levine,
1981, Copyright © 1973, 1981 by Prayer Book Press of Media Judaica Inc.
Simon & Schuster Inc, a division of Gulf & Western Corporation, for permission to
quote from CATCH-22 by Joseph Heller, 1961, Copyright © 1955, 1961 by Joseph
Heller.
Houghton Mifflin Company for permission to quote from J. B., A Play in Verse, by
Archibald MacLeish. Copyright © 1956, 1957, 1958 by Archibald MacLeish.

IN MEMORY OF
AARON ZEV KUSHNER
1963–1977

And David said: While the child was yet alive, I fasted and wept, for I said, Who knows whether the Lord will be gracious to me and the child will live. But now that he is dead, why should I fast? Can I bring him back again? I shall go to him, but he will not return to me. (II Samuel 12:22–23)

CONTENTS

WHEN
BAD THINGS
HAPPEN
TO
GOOD PEOPLE

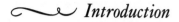

WHY
I WROTE
THIS BOOK

T‍HIS is not an abstract book about God and theology. It does not try to use big words or clever ways of rephrasing questions in an effort to convince us that our problems are not really problems, but that we only think they are. This is a very personal book, written by someone who believes in God and in the goodness of the world, someone who has spent most of his life trying to help other people believe, and was compelled by a personal tragedy to rethink everything he had been taught about God and God's ways.

Our son Aaron had just passed his third birthday when our daughter Ariel was born. Aaron was a bright and happy child, who before the age of two could identify a dozen different varieties of dinosaur and could patiently explain to an adult that dinosaurs were extinct. My wife and I had been concerned about his health from the time he stopped gaining weight at the age of eight months, and from the time his hair started falling out after he turned one year old. Prominent doctors had seen him, had attached complicated names to his condition, and had assured us that he would grow to be very

1

short but would be normal in all other ways. Just before our daughter's birth, we moved from New York to a suburb of Boston, where I became the rabbi of the local congregation. We discovered that the local pediatrician was doing research in problems of children's growth, and we introduced him to Aaron. Two months later—the day our daughter was born —he visited my wife in the hospital, and told us that our son's condition was called progeria, "rapid aging." He went on to say that Aaron would never grow much beyond three feet in height, would have no hair on his head or body, would look like a little old man while he was still a child, and would die in his early teens.

How does one handle news like that? I was a young, inexperienced rabbi, not as familiar with the process of grief as I would later come to be, and what I mostly felt that day was a deep, aching sense of unfairness. It didn't make sense. I had been a good person. I had tried to do what was right in the sight of God. More than that, I was living a more religiously committed life than most people I knew, people who had large, healthy families. I believed that I was following God's ways and doing His work. How could this be happening to my family? If God existed, if He was minimally fair, let alone loving and forgiving, how could He do this to me?

And even if I could persuade myself that I deserved this punishment for some sin of neglect or pride that I was not aware of, on what grounds did Aaron have to suffer? He was an innocent child, a happy, outgoing three-year-old. Why should he have to suffer physical and psychological pain every day of his life? Why should he have to be stared at, pointed at,

2

wherever he went? Why should he be condemned to grow into adolescence, see other boys and girls beginning to date, and realize that he would never know marriage or fatherhood? It simply didn't make sense.

Like most people, my wife and I had grown up with an image of God as an all-wise, all-powerful parent figure who would treat us as our earthly parents did, or even better. If we were obedient and deserving, He would reward us. If we got out of line, He would discipline us, reluctantly but firmly. He would protect us from being hurt or from hurting ourselves, and would see to it that we got what we deserved in life.

Like most people, I was aware of the human tragedies that darkened the landscape—the young people who died in car crashes, the cheerful, loving people wasted by crippling diseases, the neighbors and relatives whose retarded or mentally ill children people spoke of in hushed tones. But that awareness never drove me to wonder about God's justice, or to question His fairness. I assumed that He knew more about the world than I did.

Then came that day in the hospital when the doctor told us about Aaron and explained what progeria meant. It contradicted everything I had been taught. I could only repeat over and over again in my mind, "This can't be happening. It is not how the world is supposed to work." Tragedies like this were supposed to happen to selfish, dishonest people whom I, as a rabbi, would then try to comfort by assuring them of God's forgiving love. How could it be happening to me, to my son, if what I believed about the world was true?

I read recently about an Israeli mother who, every year on her son's birthday, would leave the birthday party, go into the privacy of her bedroom, and cry, because her son was now one year closer to military service, one year closer to putting his life in danger, possibly one year closer to making her one of the thousands of Israeli parents who would have to stand at the grave of a child fallen in battle. I read that, and I knew exactly how she felt. Every year, on Aaron's birthday, my wife and I would celebrate. We would rejoice in his growing up and growing in skill. But we would be gripped by the cold foreknowledge that another year's passing brought us closer to the day when he would be taken from us.

I knew then that one day I would write this book. I would write it out of my own need to put into words some of the most important things I have come to believe and know. And I would write it to help other people who might one day find themselves in a similar predicament. I would write it for all those people who wanted to go on believing, but whose anger at God made it hard for them to hold on to their faith and be comforted by religion. And I would write it for all those people whose love for God and devotion to Him led them to blame themselves for their suffering and persuade themselves that they deserved it.

There were not many books, as there were not many people, to help us when Aaron was living and dying. Friends tried, and were helpful, but how much could they really do? And the books I turned to were more concerned with defending God's honor, with logical proof that bad is really good and that evil is necessary to make this a good world, than they were with curing the bewilderment and the anguish of the parent of a dying child. They had answers to all of their own questions, but no answer for mine.

I hope that this book is not like those. I did not set out to write a book that would defend or explain God. There is no need to duplicate the many treatises already on the shelves, and even if there were, I am not a formally trained philosopher. I am fundamentally a religious man who has been hurt by life, and I wanted to write a book that could be given to the person who has been hurt by life—by death, by illness or injury, by rejection or disappointment—and who knows in his heart that if there is justice in the world, he deserved better. What can God mean to such a person? Where can he turn for strength and hope? If you are such a person, if you want to believe in God's goodness and fairness but find it hard because of the things that have happened to you and to people you care about, and if this book helps you do that, then I will have succeeded in distilling some blessing out of Aaron's pain and tears.

If I ever find my book bogging down in technical theological explanations and ignoring the human pain which should be its subject, I hope that the memory of why I set out to write it will pull me back on course. Aaron died two days after his fourteenth birthday. This is his book, because any attempt to make sense of the world's pain and evil will be judged a success or a failure based on whether it offers an acceptable explanation of why he and we had to undergo what we did. And it is his book in another sense as well—because his life made it possible, and because his death made it necessary.

～1

WHY DO
THE RIGHTEOUS
SUFFER?

THERE is only one question which really matters: why do bad things happen to good people? All other theological conversation is intellectually diverting; somewhat like doing the crossword puzzle in the Sunday paper and feeling very satisfied when you have made the words fit; but ultimately without the capacity to reach people where they really care. Virtually every meaningful conversation I have ever had with people on the subject of God and religion has either started with this question, or gotten around to it before long. Not only the troubled man or woman who has just come from a discouraging diagnosis at the doctor's office, but the college student who tells me that he has decided there is no God, or the total stranger who comes up to me at a party just when I am ready to ask the hostess for my coat, and says, "I hear you're a rabbi; how can you believe that . . ." —they all have one thing in common. They are all troubled by the unfair distribution of suffering in the world.

The misfortunes of good people are not only a problem to the people who suffer and to their families. They are a problem to everyone who wants to believe in a just and fair and livable world. They inevitably raise questions about the goodness, the kindness, even the existence of God.

I am the rabbi of a congregation of six hundred families, or about twenty-five hundred people. I visit them in the hospital, I officiate at their funerals, I try to help them through the wrenching pain of their divorces, their business failures, their unhappiness with their children. I sit and listen to them pour out their stories of terminally ill husbands or wives, of senile parents for whom a long life is a curse rather than a blessing, of seeing people whom they love contorted with pain or buried by frustration. And I find it very hard to tell them that life is fair, that God gives people what they deserve and need. Time after time, I have seen families and even whole communities unite in prayer for the recovery of a sick person, only to have their hopes and prayers mocked. I have seen the wrong people get sick, the wrong people be hurt, the wrong people die young.

Like every reader of this book, I pick up the daily paper and fresh challenges to the idea of the world's goodness assault my eyes: senseless murders, fatal practical jokes, young people killed in automobile accidents on the way to their wedding or coming home from their high school prom. I add these stories to the personal tragedies I have known, and I have to ask myself: Can I, in good faith, continue to teach people that the world is good, and that a kind and loving God is responsible for what happens in it?

People don't have to be unusual, saintly human beings to make us confront this problem. We may not often find ourselves wondering, "why do totally unselfish people suffer, people who never do anything wrong?" because we come to know very few such individuals. But we often find ourselves asking why ordinary people, nice friendly neighbors, neither extraordinarily good nor extraordinarily bad, should suddenly have to face the agony of pain and tragedy. If the world were fair, they would not seem to deserve it. They are neither very much better nor very much worse than most people we know; why should their lives be so much harder? To ask "Why do the righteous suffer?" or "why do bad things happen to good people?" is not to limit our concern to the martyrdom of saints and sages, but to try to understand why ordinary people—ourselves and people around us—should have to bear extraordinary burdens of grief and pain.

I was a young rabbi just starting out in my profession, when I was called on to try to help a family through an unexpected and almost unbearable tragedy. This middle-aged couple had one daughter, a bright nineteen-year-old girl who was in her freshman year at an out-of-state college. One morning at breakfast, they received a phone call from the university infirmary. "We have some bad news for you. Your daughter collapsed while walking to class this morning. It seems a blood vessel burst in her brain. She died before we could do anything for her. We're terribly sorry."

Stunned, the parents asked a neighbor to come in to help them decide what steps to take next. The neighbor notified the synagogue, and I went over to see them that same day. I entered their home, feeling very inadequate, not knowing any words that could ease their pain. I anticipated anger, shock, grief, but I didn't expect to hear the first words they said to me: "You know, Rabbi, we didn't fast last Yom Kippur."

Why did they say that? Why did they assume that they

were somehow responsible for this tragedy? Who taught them to believe in a God who would strike down an attractive, gifted young woman without warning as punishment for someone else's ritual infraction?

One of the ways in which people have tried to make sense of the world's suffering in every generation has been by assuming that we deserve what we get, that somehow our misfortunes come as punishment for our sins:

> Tell the righteous it shall be well with them, for they shall eat the fruit of their deeds. Woe to the wicked, it shall be ill with him, for what his hands have done shall be done to him. (*Isaiah 3:10–11*)

> But Er, Judah's first-born, was wicked in the sight of the Lord, and the Lord slew him. (*Genesis 38:7*)

> No ills befall the righteous, but the wicked are filled with trouble. (*Proverbs 12:21*)

> Consider, what innocent ever perished, or where have the righteous been destroyed? (*Job 14:7*)

This is an attitude we will meet later in the book when we discuss the whole question of guilt. It is tempting at one level to believe that bad things happen to people (especially other people) because God is a righteous judge who gives them exactly what they deserve. By believing that, we keep the world orderly and understandable. We give people the best possible reason for being good and for avoiding sin. And by believing that, we can maintain an image of God as all-loving, all-powerful and totally in control. Given the reality of human nature, given the fact that none of us is perfect and that each of us can, without too much difficulty, think of

9

things he has done which he should not have done, we can always find grounds for justifying what happens to us. But how comforting, how religiously adequate, is such an answer?

The couple whom I tried to comfort, the parents who had lost their only child at age nineteen with no warning, were not profoundly religious people. They were not active in the synagogue; they had not even fasted on Yom Kippur, a tradition which even many otherwise nonobservant Jews maintain. But when they were stunned by tragedy, they reverted back to the basic belief that God punishes people for their sins. They sat there feeling that their daughter's death had been their fault; had they been less selfish and less lazy about the Yom Kippur fast some six months earlier, she might still be alive. They sat there angry at God for having exacted His pound of flesh so strictly, but afraid to admit their anger for fear that He would punish them again. Life had hurt them, and religion could not comfort them. Religion was making them feel worse.

The idea that God gives people what they deserve, that our misdeeds cause our misfortune, is a neat and attractive solution to the problem of evil at several levels, but it has a number of serious limitations. As we have seen, it teaches people to blame themselves. It creates guilt even where there is no basis for guilt. It makes people hate God, even as it makes them hate themselves. And most disturbing of all, it does not even fit the facts.

Perhaps if we had lived before the era of mass communications, we could have believed this thesis, as many intelligent people of those centuries did. It was easier to believe then. You needed to ignore fewer cases of bad things happening to good people. Without newspapers and television, without history books, you could shrug off the occasional death of a child or of a saintly neighbor. We know too much about the world to do that today. How can anyone who recognizes the names Auschwitz and My Lai, or has walked the corridors of hospitals and nursing homes, dare to answer the question of the world's suffering by quoting Isaiah: "Tell the righteous it shall be well with them"? To believe that today, a person would either have to deny the facts that press upon him from every side, or else define what he means by "righteous" in order to fit the inescapable facts. We would have to say that a righteous person was anyone who lived long and well, whether or not he was honest and charitable, and a wicked person was anyone who suffered, even if that person's life was otherwise commendable.

A true story: an eleven-year-old boy of my acquaintance was given a routine eye examination at school and found to be just nearsighted enough to require glasses. No one was terribly surprised at the news. His parents both wear glasses, as does his older sister. But for some reason, the boy was deeply upset at the prospect, and would not tell anyone why. Finally, one night as his mother was putting him to bed, the story came out. A week before the eye examination, the boy and two older friends were looking through a pile of trash that a neighbor had set out for collection, and found a copy of the magazine *Playboy*. With a sense that they were doing something naughty, they spent several minutes looking at the pictures of unclothed women. When, a few days later, the boy failed the eye test at school and was found to need glasses, he jumped to the conclusion that God had begun the process of

11

punishing him with blindness for looking at those pictures.

Sometimes we try to make sense of life's trials by saying that people do in fact get what they deserve, but only over the course of time. At any given moment, life may seem unfair and innocent people may appear to be suffering. But if we wait long enough, we believe, we will see the righteousness of God's plan emerge.

So, for example, the Ninety-second Psalm praises God for the wonderful, flawlessly righteous world He has given us, and hints that foolish people find fault with it because they are impatient and don't give God the time it takes for His justice to emerge.

> How great are Your deeds, O Lord,
> Your thoughts are very deep.
> The ignorant man does not comprehend them,
> Nor does the fool understand them.
> When the wicked spring up like grass,
> And workers of iniquity flourish,
> It is that they may be destroyed forever. . . .
> The righteous shall flourish like the palm tree,
> And grow mighty like a cedar of Lebanon. . . .
> To declare that the Lord is upright,
> My Rock in Whom there is no unrighteousness.
> *(Psalm 92:6–8, 13, 16)*

The psalmist wants to explain the world's apparent evil as in no way compromising God's justice and righteousness. He does it by comparing the wicked to grass, and the righteous to a palm tree or cedar. If you plant grass seed and a palm tree seed on the same day, the grass will start to sprout much sooner. At that point, a person who knew nothing about nature might predict that the grass would ultimately grow to be higher and stronger than the palm tree, since it was growing faster. But the experienced observer would know that the head start of the grass was only temporary, that it would wither and die in a few months, while the tree would grow slowly, but would grow to be tall and straight and would last for more than a generation.

So too, the psalmist suggests, foolish impatient people see the prosperity of the wicked and the suffering of the upright, and jump to the conclusion that it pays to be wicked. Let them observe the situation over the long run, he notes, and they will see the wicked wither like the grass, and the righteous prosper slowly but surely, like the palm tree or cedar.

If I could meet the author of the Ninety-second Psalm, I would first congratulate him on having composed a master-piece of devotional literature. I would acknowledge that he has said something perceptive and important about the world we live in, that being dishonest and unscrupulous often gives people a head start, but that justice catches up to them. As Rabbi Milton Steinberg has written, "Consider the pattern of human affairs: how falsehood, having no legs, cannot stand; how evil tends to destroy itself; how every tyranny has eventually invoked its own doom. Now set against this the staying power of truth and righteousness. Could the contrast be so sharp unless something in the scheme of things discouraged evil and favored the good?" (*Anatomy of Faith*)

But having said that, I would be obliged to point out that there is a lot of wishful thinking in his theology. Even if I were to grant that wicked people don't get away with their wickedness, that they pay for it in one way or another, I cannot say Amen to his claim that "the righteous flourish like the palm tree." The psalmist would have us believe that, given enough time, the righteous will catch up and surpass the wicked in attaining the good things of life. How does he explain the fact that God, who is presumably behind this arrangement, does not always give the righteous man time to catch up? Some good people die unfulfilled; others find length of days to be more of a punishment than a privilege. The world, alas, is not so neat a place as the psalmist would have us believe.

I think of an acquaintance of mine who built up a modestly successful business through many years of hard work, only to be driven into bankruptcy when he was cheated by a man he had trusted. I can tell him that the victory of evil over good is only temporary, that the other person's evil ways will catch up to him. But in the meantime, my acquaintance is a tired, frustrated man, no longer young, and grown cynical about the world. Who will send his children to college, who will pay the medical bills that go with advancing age, during the years it takes for God's justice to catch up with him? No matter how much I would like to believe, with Milton Steinberg, that justice will ultimately emerge, can I guarantee that he will live long enough to see himself vindicated? I find I cannot share the optimism of the psalmist that the righteous, in the long run, will flourish like the palm tree and give testimony to God's uprightness.

Often, victims of misfortune try to console themselves with the idea that God has His reasons for making this happen to them, reasons that they are in no position to judge. I think of a woman I know named Helen.

The trouble started when Helen noticed herself getting tired after walking several blocks or standing in line. She chalked it up to getting older and having put on some weight. But one night, coming home after dinner with friends, Helen stumbled over the threshold of the front door, sent a lamp crashing to the floor, and fell to the floor herself. Her husband tried to joke about her getting drunk on two sips of wine, but Helen suspected that it was no joking matter. The following morning, she made an appointment to see a doctor.

The diagnosis was multiple sclerosis. The doctor explained that it was a degenerative nerve disease, and that it would gradually get worse, maybe quickly, maybe gradually over many years. At some point Helen would find it harder to walk without support. Eventually she would be confined to a wheelchair, lose bowel and bladder control, and become more and more of an invalid until she died.

The worst of Helen's fears had come true. She broke down and cried when she heard that. "Why should this happen to me? I've tried to be a good person. I have a husband and young children who need me. I don't deserve this. Why should God make me suffer like this?" Her husband took her hand and tried to console her: "You can't talk like that. God must have His reasons for doing this, and it's not for us to question Him. You have to believe that if He wants you to get better, you will get better, and if He doesn't, there has to be some purpose to it."

Helen tried to find peace and strength in those words. She wanted to be comforted by the knowledge that there was some purpose to her suffering, beyond her capacity to understand. She wanted to believe that it made sense at some level. All her life, she had been taught—at religious school and in science classes alike—that the world made sense, that everything that happened, happened for a reason. She wanted so desperately to go on believing that, to hold on to her belief that God was in charge of things, because if He wasn't, who was? It was hard to live with multiple sclerosis, but it was even harder to live with the idea that things happened to people for no reason, that God had lost touch with the world and nobody was in the driver's seat.

Helen didn't want to question God or be angry at Him. But her husband's words only made her feel more abandoned and more bewildered. What kind of higher purpose could possibly justify what she would have to face? How could this in any way be good? Much as she tried not to be angry at God, she felt angry, hurt, betrayed. She had been a good person; not perfect, perhaps, but honest, hard-working, helpful, as good as most people and better than many who were walking around healthy. What reasons could God possibly have for doing this to her? And on top of it all, she felt guilty for being angry at God. She felt alone in her fear and suffering. If God had sent her this affliction, if He, for some reason, wanted her to suffer, how could she ask Him to cure her of it?

In 1924 the novelist Thornton Wilder attempted to confront this question of questions in his novel *The Bridge of San Luis Rey*. One day in a small town in Peru, a rope bridge over a chasm breaks and the five people who are crossing the bridge fall to their deaths. A young Catholic priest happens to be watching, and is troubled by the event. Was it sheer accident, or was it somehow God's will that those five people should die that way? He investigates their life stories, and comes to an enigmatic conclusion: all five had recently resolved a problematic situation in their lives and were now about to enter a new phase. Perhaps it *was* an appropriate time for each of them to die, thinks the priest.

I confess that I find that answer ultimately unsatisfying. For Wilder's five pedestrians on a rope bridge, let us substitute two hundred and fifty passengers on an airplane that crashes. It strains the imagination to claim that every single one of them had just passed a point of resolution in his life. The human-interest stories in the newspapers after a plane crash seem to indicate the opposite—that many of the victims were in the middle of important work, that many left young families and unfulfilled plans. In a novel, where the author's imagination can control the facts, sudden tragedies can happen to people when the plot calls for it. But experience has taught me that real life is not all that neat.

It may be that Thornton Wilder came to that conclusion himself. More than forty years after writing *The Bridge of San Luis Rey*, an older and wiser Wilder returned to the question of why good people suffer in another novel, *The Eighth Day*. The book tells the story of a good and decent man whose life is ruined by bad luck and hostility. He and his family suffer although they are innocent. At the end of the novel, where the reader would hope for a happy ending, with heroes rewarded and villains punished, there is none. Instead, Wilder offers us the image of a beautiful tapestry. Looked at from the right side, it is an intricately woven work of art, drawing together threads of different lengths and colors to make up an inspiring picture. But turn the tapestry over, and you will see a hodgepodge of many threads, some short and some long, some smooth and some cut and knotted, going off in different directions. Wilder offers this as his explanation of why good people have to suffer in this life. God has a pattern into which all of our lives fit. His pattern requires that some lives be twisted, knotted, or cut short, while others extend to impressive lengths, not because one thread is more deserving than another, but simply because the pattern requires it. Looked at from underneath, from our vantage point in life, God's pattern of reward and punishment seems arbitrary and without design, like the underside of a tapestry. But looked at from outside this life, from God's vantage point, every twist and knot is seen to have its place in a great design that adds up to a work of art.

There is much that is moving in this suggestion, and I can imagine that many people would find it comforting. Pointless suffering, suffering as punishment for some unspecified sin, is hard to bear. But suffering as a contribution to a great work of art designed by God Himself may be seen, not only as a tolerable burden, but even as a privilege. So one victim of medieval misfortune is supposed to have prayed, "Tell me not why I must suffer. Assure me only that I suffer for Thy sake."

On closer examination, however, this approach is found wanting. For all its compassion, it too is based in large measure on wishful thinking. The crippling illness of a child, the death of a young husband and father, the ruin of an innocent person through malicious gossip—these are all real. We have seen them. But nobody has seen Wilder's tapestry. All he can say to us is "Imagine that there might be such a tapestry." I find it very hard to accept hypothetical solutions to real problems.

How seriously would we take a person who said, "I have faith in Adolf Hitler, or in John Dillinger. I can't explain why they did the things they did, but I can't believe they would have done them without a good reason." Yet people try to justify the deaths and tragedies God inflicts on innocent victims with almost these same words.

Furthermore, my religious commitment to the supreme value of an individual life makes it hard for me to accept an answer that is not scandalized by an innocent person's pain, that condones human pain because it supposedly contributes to an overall work of esthetic value. If a human artist or employer made children suffer so that something immensely impressive or valuable could come to pass, we would put him in prison. Why then should we excuse God for causing such undeserved pain, no matter how wonderful the ultimate result may be?

Helen, contemplating a life of physical pain and mental anguish, finds that her illness has robbed her of her childhood faith in God and in the goodness of the world. She challenges her family, her friends, her clergyman, to explain why such a terrible thing should happen to her, or for that matter to anyone. If there really is a God, says Helen, she hates Him, and hates whatever "grand design" caused Him to inflict such misery on her.

Let us now consider another question: Can suffering be educational? Can it cure us of our faults and make us better people? Sometimes religious people who would like to believe that God has good reasons for making us suffer, try to imagine what those reasons might be. In the words of one of the great Orthodox Jewish teachers of our time, Rabbi Joseph B.

Soloveitchik, "Suffering comes to ennoble man, to purge his thoughts of pride and superficiality, to expand his horizons. In sum, the purpose of suffering is to repair that which is faulty in a man's personality."

Just as a parent sometimes has to punish a child whom he loves, for the child's sake, so God has to punish us. A parent who pulls his child out of a busy roadway, or refuses to give him a candy bar before supper, is not being mean or punitive or unfair. He or she is just being a concerned, responsible parent. Sometimes a parent even has to punish a child, with a spanking or a deprivation, in order to drive home a lesson. The child may feel that he is being arbitrarily deprived of something all the other children have, and he may wonder why an ostensibly loving parent should treat him that way, but that is because he is still a child. When he grows up, he will come to understand the wisdom and necessity of it.

Similarly, we are told, God treats us the way a wise and caring parent treats a naive child, keeping us from hurting ourselves, withholding something we may think we want, punishing us occasionally to make sure we understand that we have done something seriously wrong, and patiently enduring our temper tantrums at His "unfairness" in the confidence that we will one day mature and understand that it was all for our own good. "For whom the Lord loves, He chastises, even as a father does to the son he loves." (Proverbs 3:12)

The newspapers recently carried the story of a woman who had spent six years traveling around the world buying antiques, preparing to set up a business. A week before she was ready to open, a wayward bolt of lightning set off an electrical fire in a block of stores, and several shops, including hers, were burned down. The goods, being priceless and irreplaceable, were insured for only a fraction of their value. And what insurance settlement could compensate a middle-aged woman for six years of her life spent in searching and collecting? The poor woman was distraught. "Why did this have to happen? Why did it happen to me?" One friend, trying to console her, was quoted as saying, "Maybe God is trying to teach you a lesson. Maybe He is trying to tell you that He doesn't want you to be rich. He doesn't want you to be a successful businesswoman, caught up in profit-and-loss statements all day long and annual trips to the Far East to buy things. He wants you to put your energies into something else, and this was His way of getting His message across to you."

A contemporary teacher has used this image: if a man who knew nothing about medicine were to walk into the operating room of a hospital and see doctors and nurses performing an operation, he might assume that they were a band of criminals torturing their unfortunate victim. He would see them tying the patient down, forcing a cone over his nose and mouth so that he could not breathe, and sticking knives and needles into him. Only someone who understood surgery would realize that they were doing all this to help the patient, not to torment him. So too, it is suggested, God does painful things to us as His way of helping us.

Consider the case of Ron, a young pharmacist who ran a drugstore with an older partner. When Ron bought into the business, his older colleague told him that the store had recently been the target of a series of holdups by young drug addicts looking for drugs and cash. One day, when Ron was

21

almost ready to close up, a teenage junkie pulled a small-caliber handgun on him and asked for drugs and money. Ron was willing to lose a day's receipts rather than try to be a hero. He went to open the cash register, his hands trembling as he did so. As he turned, he stumbled and reached for the counter to brace himself. The robber thought he was going for a gun, and fired. The bullet went through Ron's abdomen and lodged in his spinal cord. Doctors removed it, but the damage had been done. Ron would never walk again.

Friends tried to console him. Some held his hand and commiserated with him. Some told him of experimental drugs doctors were using on paraplegics, or of miraculous spontaneous recoveries they had read about. Others tried to help him understand what had happened to him, and to answer his question, "Why me?"

"I have to believe," one friend said, "that everything that happens in life, happens for a purpose. Somehow or other, everything that happens to us is meant for our good. Look at it this way. You were always a pretty cocky guy, popular with girls, flashy cars, confident you were going to make a lot of money. You never really took time to worry about the people who couldn't keep up with you. Maybe this is God's way of teaching you a lesson, making you more thoughtful, more sensitive to others. Maybe this is God's way of purging you of pride and arrogance, and thinking about how you were going to be such a success. It's His way of making you a better, more sensitive person."

The friend wanted to be comforting, to make sense of this senseless accident. But if you were Ron, what would your reaction have been? Ron remembers thinking that if he hadn't been confined to a hospital bed, he would have punched the other man. What right did a normal, healthy person—a person who would soon be driving home, walking upstairs, looking forward to playing tennis—have to tell him that what had happened to him was good and was in his best interest?

The problem with a line of reasoning like this one is that it isn't really meant to help the sufferer or to explain his suffering. It is meant primarily to defend God, to use words and ideas to transform bad into good and pain into privilege. Such answers are thought up by people who believe very strongly that God is a loving parent who controls what happens to us, and on the basis of that belief adjust and interpret the facts to fit their assumption. It may be true that surgeons stick knives into people to help them, but not everyone who sticks a knife into somebody else is a surgeon. It may be true that sometimes we have to do painful things to people we love for their benefit, but not every painful thing that happens to us is beneficial.

I would find it easier to believe that I experience tragedy and suffering in order to "repair" that which is faulty in my personality if there were some clear connection between the fault and the punishment. A parent who disciplines a child for doing something wrong, but never tells him what he is being punished for, is hardly a model of responsible parenthood. Yet, those who explain suffering as God's way of teaching us to change are at a loss to specify just what it is about us we are supposed to change.

Equally unhelpful would be the explanation that Ron's accident happened not to make *him* a more sensitive person, but to make his friends and family more sensitive to the handicapped than they would otherwise have been. Perhaps women give birth to dwarfed or retarded children as part of God's plan to deepen and enlarge their souls, to teach them compassion and a different kind of love.

We have all read stories of little children who were left unwatched for just a moment and fell from a window or into a swimming pool and died. Why does God permit such a thing to happen to an innocent child? It can't be to teach a child a lesson about exploring new areas. By the time the lesson is over, the child is dead. Is it to teach the parents and baby-sitters to be more careful? That is too trivial a lesson to be purchased at the price of a child's life. Is it to make the parents more sensitive, more compassionate people, more appreciative of life and health because of their experience? Is it to move them to work for better safety standards, and in that way save a hundred future lives? The price is still too high, and the reasoning shows too little regard for the value of an individual life. I am offended by those who suggest that God creates retarded children so that those around them will learn compassion and gratitude. Why should God distort someone else's life to such a degree in order to enhance my spiritual sensitivity?

If we cannot satisfactorily explain suffering by saying we deserve what we get, or by viewing it as a "cure" for our faults, can we accept the interpretation of tragedy as a test? Many parents of dying children are urged to read the twenty-second chapter of the Book of Genesis to help them understand and accept their burden. In that chapter, God orders Abraham to take his son Isaac, whom he loves, and offer him to God as a human sacrifice. The chapter begins with the words "It came to pass after all these matters that the Lord tested Abraham." God had Abraham go through that ordeal to test his loyalty and the strength of his faith. When he passed the test, God promised to reward him liberally for the strength he had shown.

For those who have difficulty with the notion of a God who plays such sadistic games with His most faithful follower, proponents of this view explain that God knows how the story will end. He knows that we will pass the test, as Abraham did, with our faith intact (though, in Abraham's case, the child did not die). He puts us to the test so that *we* will discover how strong and faithful we are.

The Talmud, the compilation of the teachings of the rabbis between the years 200 B.C. and A.D. 500, explains Abraham's test this way: If you go to the marketplace, you will see the potter hitting his clay pots with a stick to show how strong and solid they are. But the wise potter hits only the strongest pots, never the flawed ones. So too, God sends such tests and afflictions only to people He knows are capable of handling them, so that they and others can learn the extent of their spiritual strength.

I was the parent of a handicapped child for fourteen years, until his death. I was not comforted by this notion that God had singled me out because He recognized some special spiritual strength within me and knew that I would be able to handle it better. It didn't make me feel "privileged," nor did it help me understand why God has to send handicapped children into the lives of a hundred thousand unsuspecting families every year.

Writer Harriet Sarnoff Schiff has distilled her pain and

tragedy into an excellent book, *The Bereaved Parent*. She remembers that when her young son died during an operation to correct a congenital heart malfunction, her clergyman took her aside and said, "I know that this is a painful time for you. But I know that you will get through it all right, because God never sends us more of a burden than we can bear. God only let this happen to you because He knows that you are strong enough to handle it." Harriet Schiff remembers her reaction to those words: "If only I was a weaker person, Robbie would still be alive."

Does God "temper the wind to the shorn lamb"? Does He never ask more of us than we can endure? My experience, alas, has been otherwise. I have seen people crack under the strain of unbearable tragedy. I have seen marriages break up after the death of a child, because parents blamed each other for not taking proper care or for carrying the defective gene, or simply because the memories they shared were unendurably painful. I have seen some people made noble and sensitive through suffering, but I have seen many more people grow cynical and bitter. I have seen people become jealous of those around them, unable to take part in the routines of normal living. I have seen cancers and automobile accidents take the life of one member of a family, and functionally end the lives of five others, who could never again be the normal, cheerful people they were before disaster struck. If God is testing us, He must know by now that many of us fail the test. If He is only giving us burdens we can bear, I have seen Him miscalculate far too often.

When all else fails, some people try to explain suffering by believing that it comes to liberate us from a world of pain and lead us to a better place. I received a phone call one day informing me that a five-year-old boy in our neighborhood had run out into the street after a ball, had been hit by a car and killed. I didn't know the boy; his family was not part of the congregation. But several children from the congregation had known him and played with him. Their mothers attended the funeral, and some of them told me about it afterwards.

In the eulogy, the family's clergyman had said, "This is not a time for sadness or tears. This is a time for rejoicing, because Michael has been taken out of this world of sin and pain with his innocent soul unstained by sin. He is in a happier land now where there is no pain and no grief; let us thank God for that."

I heard that, and I felt so bad for Michael's parents. Not only had they lost a child without warning, they were being told by the representative of their religion that they should rejoice in the fact that he had died so young and so innocent, and I couldn't believe that they felt much like rejoicing at that moment. They felt hurt, they felt angry, they felt that God had been unfair to them, and here was God's spokesman telling them to be grateful to God for what had happened.

Sometimes in our reluctance to admit that there is unfairness in the world, we try to persuade ourselves that what has happened is not really bad. We only think that it is. It is only our selfishness that makes us cry because five-year-old Michael is with God instead of living with us. Sometimes, in our cleverness, we try to persuade ourselves that what we call evil is not real, does not really exist, but is only a condition of not enough goodness, even as "cold" means "not enough heat," or darkness is a name we give to the absence of light.

27

We may thus "prove" that there is really no such thing as darkness or cold, but people do stumble and hurt themselves because of the dark, and people do die of exposure to cold. Their deaths and injuries are no less real because of our verbal cleverness.

Sometimes, because our souls yearn for justice, because we so desperately want to believe that God will be fair to us, we fasten our hopes on the idea that life in this world is not the only reality. Somewhere beyond this life is another world where "the last shall be first" and those whose lives were cut short here on earth will be reunited with those they loved, and will spend eternity with them.

Neither I nor any other living person can know anything about the reality of that hope. We know that our physical bodies decay after we die. I for one believe that the part of us which is not physical, the part we call the soul or personality, does not and cannot die. But I am not capable of imagining what a soul without a body looks like. Will we be able to recognize disembodied souls as being the people we had known and loved? Will a man who lost his father at a young age, and then lived a full life, be older, younger, or the same age as his father in the world-to-come? Will the souls of the retarded or the short-tempered be somehow made whole in Heaven?

People who have been close to death and recovered tell of seeing a bright light and being greeted by someone they had loved, now deceased. After our son's death, our daughter dreamed that she had died and was welcomed into Heaven by her brother, now grown normal, and by her grandmother (who had died the year before). Needless to say, we have no way of knowing whether these visions are intimations of reality or products of our own wishful thinking.

Belief in a world to come where the innocent are compensated for their suffering can help people endure the unfairness of life in this world without losing faith. But it can also be an excuse for not being troubled or outraged by injustice around us, and not using our God-given intelligence to try to do something about it. The dictate of practical wisdom for people in our situation might be to remain mindful of the possibility that our lives continue in some form after death, perhaps in a form our earthly imaginations cannot conceive of. But at the same time, since we cannot know for sure, we would be well advised to take this world as seriously as we can, in case it turns out to be the only one we will ever have, and to look for meaning and justice here.

All the responses to tragedy which we have considered have at least one thing in common. They all assume that God is the cause of our suffering, and they try to understand why God would want us to suffer. Is it for our own good, or is it a punishment we deserve, or could it be that God does not care what happens to us? Many of the answers were sensitive and imaginative, but none was totally satisfying. Some led us to blame ourselves in order to spare God's reputation. Others asked us to deny reality or to repress our true feelings. We were left either hating ourselves for deserving such a fate, or hating God for sending it to us when we did not deserve it.

There may be another approach. Maybe God does not cause our suffering. Maybe it happens for some reason other than the will of God. The psalmist writes, "I lift mine eyes to the hills; from where does my help come? My help comes from the Lord, maker of Heaven and earth." (Psalm 121:1–2) He does not say, "My pain comes from the Lord," or "my tragedy comes from the Lord." He says "my *help* comes from the Lord."

Could it be that God does not cause the bad things that happen to us? Could it be that He doesn't decide which families shall give birth to a handicapped child, that He did not single out Ron to be crippled by a bullet or Helen by a degenerative disease, but rather that He stands ready to help them and us cope with our tragedies if we could only get beyond the feelings of guilt and anger that separate us from Him? Could it be that "How could God do this to me?" is really the wrong question for us to ask?

The most profound and complete consideration of human suffering in the Bible, perhaps in all of literature, is the Book of Job. It is to an examination of that book that we now turn.

THE STORY OF A MAN NAMED JOB

About twenty-five hundred years ago, a man lived whose name we will never know, but who has enriched the minds and lives of human beings ever since. He was a sensitive man who saw good people getting sick and dying around him while proud and selfish people prospered. He heard all the learned, clever, and pious attempts to explain life, and he was as dissatisfied with them as we are today. Because he was a person of rare literary and intellectual gifts, he wrote a long philosophical poem on the subject of why God lets bad things happen to good people. This poem appears in the Bible as the Book of Job.

Thomas Carlyle called the Book of Job "the most wonderful poem of any age and language; our first, oldest statement of the never-ending problem—man's destiny and God's way with him here in this earth. . . . There is nothing written in the Bible or out of it of equal literary merit." I have been fascinated by the Book of Job ever since I learned of its existence, and have studied it, reread it, and taught it any number of times. It has been said that just as every actor yearns to play Hamlet, every Bible student yearns to write a commentary on the Book of Job. It is a hard book to understand, a profound and beautiful book on the most profound of subjects, the question of why God lets good people suffer. Its argument is hard to follow because, through some of the characters, the author presents views he himself probably did not accept, and because he wrote in an elegant Hebrew which, thousands of years later, is often hard to translate. If you compare two English translations of Job, you may wonder if they are both translations of the same book. One of the key verses can be taken to mean either "I will fear God" or "I will not fear God," and there is no way of knowing for sure what the author intended. The familiar statement of faith "I know that my Redeemer lives" may mean instead "I would rather be redeemed while I am still alive." But much of the book is clear and forceful, and we can try our interpretive skills on the rest.

Who was Job, and what is the book that bears his name? A long, long time ago, scholars believe, there must have been a well-known folk story, a kind of morality fable told to reinforce people's religious sentiments, about a pious man named Job. Job was so good, so perfect, that you realize at once that you are not reading about a real-life person. This is a "once-upon-a-time" story about a good man who suffered.

One day, the story goes, Satan appears before God to tell Him about all the sinful things people were doing on earth. God says to Satan, "Did you notice My servant Job? There is no one on earth like him, a thoroughly good man who never sins." Satan answers God, "Of course Job is pious and obedient. You make it worth his while, showering riches and blessings on him. Take away those blessings and see how long he remains Your obedient servant."

God accepts Satan's challenge. Without in any way telling Job what is going on, God destroys Job's house and cattle and kills his children. He afflicts Job with boils all over his body, so that his every moment becomes physical torture. Job's wife urges him to curse God, even if that means God's striking him dead. He can't do anything worse to Job than He already has done. Three friends come to console Job, and they too urge him to give up his piety, if this is the reward it brings him. But Job remains steadfast in his faith. Nothing that happens to him can make him give up his devotion to God. At the end, God appears, scolds the friends for their advice, and rewards Job for his faithfulness. God gives him a new home, a new fortune, and new children. The moral of the story is: when hard times befall you, don't be tempted to give up your faith in God. He has His reasons for what He is doing, and if you hold on to your faith long enough, He will compensate you for your suffering.

Over the generations, many people must have been told that story. Some, no doubt, were comforted by it. Others were shamed into keeping their doubts and complaints to themselves after hearing Job's example. Our anonymous author was bothered by it. What kind of God would that story have us believe in, who would kill innocent children and visit unbearable anguish on His most devoted follower in order to prove a point, in order, we almost feel, to win a bet with Satan? What kind of religion is the story urging on us, which delights in blind obedience and calls it sinful to protest

33

against injustice? He was so upset with this pious old fable that he took it, turned it inside out, and recast it as a philosophical poem in which the characters' positions are reversed. In the poem, Job *does* complain against God, and now it is the friends who uphold the conventional theology, the idea that "no ills befall the righteous."

In an effort to comfort Job, whose children have died and who is suffering from the boils, the three friends say all the traditional, pious things. In essence, they preach the point of view contained in the original Job-fable: Don't lose faith, despite these calamities. We have a loving Father in Heaven, and He will see to it that the good prosper and the wicked are punished.

Job, who has probably spoken these same words innumerable times to other mourners, realizes for the first time how hollow and offensive they are. What do you mean, He will see to it that the good prosper and the wicked are punished?! Are you implying that my children were wicked and that is why they died? Are you saying that I am wicked, and that is why all this is happening to me? Where was I so terrible? What did I do that was so much worse than anything you did, that I should suffer so much worse a fate?

The friends are startled by this outburst. They respond by saying that a person can't expect God to tell him what he is being punished for. (At one point, one of the friends says, in effect, "what do you want from God, an itemized report about every time you told a lie or ignored a beggar? God is too busy running a world to invite you to go over His records with Him.") We can only assume that nobody is perfect, and that God knows what He is doing. If we don't assume that, the world becomes chaotic and unlivable.

And so that argument continues. Job doesn't claim to be perfect, but says that he has tried, more than most people, to live a good and decent life. How can God be a loving God if He is constantly spying on people, ready to pounce on any imperfection in an otherwise good record, and use that to justify punishment? And how can God be a just God if so many wicked people are not punished as horribly as Job is?

The dialogue becomes heated, even angry. The friends say: Job, you really had us fooled. You gave us the impression that you were as pious and religious as we are. But now we see how you throw religion overboard the first time something unpleasant happens to you. You are proud, arrogant, impatient, and blasphemous. No wonder God is doing this to you. It just proves our point that human beings can be fooled as to who is a saint and who is a sinner, but you can't fool God.

After three cycles of dialogue in which we alternately witness Job voicing his complaints and the friends defending God, the book comes to its thunderous climax. The author brilliantly has Job make use of a principle of biblical criminal law: if a man is accused of wrongdoing without proof, he may take an oath, swearing to his innocence. At that point, the accuser must either come up with evidence against him or drop the charges. In a long and eloquent statement that takes up chapters 29 and 30 of the biblical book, Job swears to his innocence. He claims that he never neglected the poor, never took anything that did not belong to him, never boasted of his wealth or rejoiced in his enemy's misfortune. He challenges

God to appear with evidence, or to admit that Job is right and has suffered wrongly.

And God appears.

There comes a terrible windstorm, out of the desert, and God answers Job out of the whirlwind. Job's case is so compelling, his challenge so forceful, that God Himself comes down to earth to answer him. But God's answer is hard to understand. He doesn't talk about Job's case at all, neither to detail Job's sins nor to explain his suffering. Instead, He says to Job, in effect, What do you know about how to run a world?

> Where were you when I planned the earth?
> Tell me, if you are wise.
> Do you know who took its dimensions,
> Measuring its length with a cord? . . .
> Were you there when I stopped the sea . . .
> And set its boundaries, saying, "Here you may come,
> But no further"?
> Have you seen where the snow is stored,
> Or visited the storehouse of the hail? . . .
> Do you tell the antelope when to calve?
> Do you give the horse his strength?
> Do you show the hawk how to fly?
>
> *(Job 38, 39)*

And now a very different Job answers, saying, "I put my hand to my mouth. I have said too much already; now I will speak no more."

The Book of Job is probably the greatest, fullest, most profound discussion of the subject of good people suffering ever written. Part of its greatness lies in the fact that the author was scrupulously fair to all points of view, even those he did not accept. Though his sympathies are clearly with Job, he makes sure that the speeches of the friends are as carefully thought out and as carefully written as are his hero's words. That makes for great literature, but it also makes it hard to understand his message. When God says, "How dare you challenge the way I run my world? What do you know about running a world?", is that supposed to be the last word on the subject, or is that just one more paraphrase of the conventional piety of that time?

To try to understand the book and its answer, let us take note of three statements which everyone in the book, and most of the readers, would like to be able to believe:

A. God is all-powerful and causes everything that happens in the world. Nothing happens without His willing it.

B. God is just and fair, and stands for people getting what they deserve, so that the good prosper and the wicked are punished.

C. Job is a good person.

As long as Job is healthy and wealthy, we can believe all three of those statements at the same time with no difficulty. When Job suffers, when he loses his possessions, his family and his health, we have a problem. We can no longer make sense of all three propositions together. We can now affirm any two only by denying the third.

If God is both just and powerful, then Job must be a sinner who deserves what is happening to him. If Job is good but God causes his suffering anyway, then God is not just. If Job deserved better and God did not send his suffering, then God is not all-powerful. We can see the argument of the Book of Job as an argument over which of the three statements we are prepared to sacrifice, so that we can keep on believing in the other two.

Job's friends are prepared to stop believing in (C), the assertion that Job is a good person. They want to believe in God as they have been taught to. They want to believe that God is good and that God is in control of things. And the only way they can do that is to convince themselves that Job deserves what is happening to him.

They start out truly wanting to comfort Job and make him feel better. They try to reassure him by quoting all the maxims of faith and confidence on which they and Job alike were raised. They want to comfort Job by telling him that the world does in fact make sense, that it is not a chaotic, meaningless place. What they do not realize is that they can only make sense of the world, and of Job's suffering, by deciding that he deserves what he has gone through. To say that everything works out in God's world may be comforting to the casual bystander, but it is an insult to the bereaved and the unfortunate. "Cheer up, Job, nobody ever gets anything he doesn't have coming to him" is not a very cheering message to someone in Job's circumstances.

But it is hard for the friends to say anything else. They believe, and want to continue believing, in God's goodness and power. But if Job is innocent, then God must be guilty—guilty of making an innocent man suffer. With that at stake, they find it easier to stop believing in *Job's* goodness than to stop believing in God's perfection.

It may also be that Job's comforters could not be objective

about what had happened to their friend. Their thinking may have been confused by their own reactions of guilt and relief that these misfortunes had befallen Job and not them. There is a German psychological term, *Schadenfreude*, which refers to the embarrassing reaction of relief we feel when something bad happens to someone else instead of to us. The soldier in combat who sees his friend killed twenty yards away while he himself is unhurt, the pupil who sees another child get into trouble for copying on a test—they don't wish their friends ill, but they can't help feeling an embarrassing spasm of gratitude that it happened to someone else and not to them. Like the friends who tried to comfort Ron or Helen, they hear a voice inside them saying, "It could just as easily have been me," and they try to silence it by saying, "No, that's not true. There is a reason why it happened to him and not to me."

We see this psychology at work elsewhere, blaming the victim so that evil doesn't seem quite so irrational and threatening. If the Jews had behaved differently, Hitler would not have been driven to murder them. If the young woman had not been so provocatively dressed, the man would not have assaulted her. If people worked harder, they would not be poor. If society did not taunt poor people by advertising things they cannot afford, they would not steal. Blaming the victim is a way of reassuring ourselves that the world is not as bad a place as it may seem, and that there are good reasons for people's suffering. It helps fortunate people believe that their good fortune is deserved, rather than being a matter of luck. It makes everyone feel better—except the victim, who now suffers the double abuse of social condemnation on top of his original misfortune. This is the approach of Job's friends, and

39

while it may solve their problem, it does not solve Job's, or ours.

Job, for his part, is unwilling to hold the world together theologically by admitting that he is a villain. He knows a lot of things intellectually, but he knows one thing more deeply. Job is absolutely sure that he is not a bad person. He may not be perfect, but he is not so much worse than others, by any intelligible moral standard, that he should deserve to lose his home, his children, his wealth and health while other people get to keep all those things. And he is not prepared to lie to save God's reputation.

Job's solution is to reject proposition (B), the affirmation of God's goodness. Job is in fact a good man, but God is so powerful that He is not limited by considerations of fairness and justice.

A philosopher might put it this way: God may *choose* to be fair and give a person what he deserves, punishing the wicked and rewarding the righteous. But can we say logically that an all-powerful God *must* be fair? Would He still be all-powerful if we, by living virtuous lives, could *compel* Him to protect and reward us? Or would He then be reduced to a kind of cosmic vending machine, into which we insert the right number of tokens and from which we get what we want (with the option of kicking and cursing the machine if it doesn't give us what we paid for)? An ancient sage is said to have rejoiced at the world's injustice, saying, "Now I can do God's will out of love for Him and not out of self-interest." That is, he could be a moral, obedient person out of sheer love for God, without the calculation that moral obedient people will be rewarded with good fortune. He could love God even if God did not love

40

him in return. The problem with such an answer is that it tries to promote justice and fairness and at the same time tries to celebrate God for being so great that He is beyond the limitations of justice and fairness.

Job sees God as being above notions of fairness, being so powerful that no moral rules apply to Him. God is seen as resembling an Oriental potentate, with unchallenged power over the life and property of his subjects. And in fact, the old fable of Job does picture God in just that way, as a deity who afflicts Job without any moral qualms in order to test his loyalty, and who feels that He has "made it up" to Job afterward by rewarding him lavishly. The God of the fable, held up as a figure to be worshiped for so many generations, is very much like an (insecure) ancient king, rewarding people not for their goodness but for their loyalty.

So Job constantly wishes that there were an umpire to mediate between himself and God, someone God would have to explain Himself to. But when it comes to God, he ruefully admits, there are no rules. "Behold He snatches away and who can hinder Him? Who can say to Him, What are You doing?" (Job 9:12)

How does Job understand his misery? He says, we live in an unjust world, from which we cannot expect fairness. There is a God, but He is free of the limitations of justice and righteousness.

What about the anonymous author of the book? What is his answer to the riddle of life's unfairness? As indicated, it is hard to know just what he thought and what solution he had in mind when he set out to write his book. It seems clear that he has put his answer into God's mouth in the speech from the whirlwind, coming as it does at the climax of the book. But what does it mean? Is it simply that Job is silenced by finding out that there is a God, that there really is someone in charge up there? But Job never doubted that. It was God's sympathy, accountability, and fairness that were at issue, not His existence. Is the answer that God is so powerful that He doesn't have to explain Himself to Job? But that is precisely what Job has been claiming throughout the book: There is a God, and He is so powerful that He doesn't have to be fair. What new insight does the author bring by having God appear and speak, if that is all He has to say, and why is Job so apologetic if it turns out that God agrees with him?

Is God saying, as some commentators suggest, that He has other considerations to worry about, besides the welfare of one individual human being, when He makes decisions that affect our lives? Is He saying that, from our human vantage point, our sicknesses and business failures are the most important things imaginable, but God has more on His mind than that? To say that is to say that the morality of the Bible, with its stress on human virtue and the sanctity of the individual life, is irrelevant to God, and that charity, justice, and the dignity of the individual human being have some source other than God. If that were true, many of us would be tempted to leave God, and seek out and worship that source of charity, justice, and human dignity instead.

Let me suggest that the author of the Book of Job takes the position which neither Job nor his friends take. He believes in God's goodness and in Job's goodness, and is prepared to give up his belief in proposition (A): that God is all-powerful. Bad things do happen to good people in this world, but it is not

God who wills it. God would like people to get what they deserve in life, but He cannot always arrange it. Forced to choose between a good God who is not totally powerful, or a powerful God who is not totally good, the author of the Book of Job chooses to believe in God's goodness.

The most important lines in the entire book may be the ones spoken by God in the second half of the speech from the whirlwind, chapter 40, verses 9–14:

> Have you an arm like God?
> Can you thunder with a voice like His?
> *You* tread down the wicked where they stand,
> Bury them in the dust together . . .
> Then will I acknowledge that your own right hand
> Can give you victory.

I take these lines to mean "if you think that it is so easy to keep the world straight and true, to keep unfair things from happening to people, *you* try it." God wants the righteous to live peaceful, happy lives, but sometimes even He can't bring that about. It is too difficult even for God to keep cruelty and chaos from claiming their innocent victims. But could man, without God, do it better?

The speech goes on, in chapter 41, to describe God's battle with the sea serpent Leviathan. With great effort, God is able to catch him in a net and pin him with fish hooks, but it is not easy. If the sea serpent is a symbol of chaos and evil, of all the uncontrollable things in the world (as it traditionally is in ancient mythology), the author may be saying there too that even God has a hard time keeping chaos in check and limiting the damage that evil can do.

Innocent people do suffer misfortunes in this life. Things happen to them far worse than they deserve—they lose their jobs, they get sick, their children suffer or make them suffer. But when it happens, it does not represent God punishing them for something they did wrong. The misfortunes do not come from God at all.

There may be a sense of loss at coming to this conclusion. In a way, it was comforting to believe in an all-wise, all-powerful God who guaranteed fair treatment and happy endings, who reassured us that everything happened for a reason, even as life was easier for us when we could believe that our parents were wise enough to know what tò do and strong enough to make everything turn out right. But it was comforting the way the religion of Job's friends was comforting: it worked only as long as we did not take the problems of innocent victims seriously. When we have met Job, when we have *been* Job, we cannot believe in that sort of God any longer without giving up our own right to feel angry, to feel that we have been treated badly by life.

From that perspective, there ought to be a sense of relief in coming to the conclusion that God is not doing this to us. If God is a God of justice and not of power, then He can still be on our side when bad things happen to us. He can know that we are good and honest people who deserve better. Our misfortunes are none of His doing, and so we can turn to Him for help. Our question will not be Job's question "God, why are You doing this to me?" but rather "God, see what is happening to me. Can You help me?" We will turn to God, not to be judged or forgiven, not to be rewarded or punished, but to be strengthened and comforted.

If we have grown up, as Job and his friends did, believing in an all-wise, all-powerful, all-knowing God, it will be hard for us, as it was hard for them, to change our way of thinking about Him (as it was hard for us, when we were children, to realize that our parents were not all-powerful, that a broken toy had to be thrown out because they *could not* fix it, not because they did not want to). But if we can bring ourselves to acknowledge that there are some things God does not control, many good things become possible.

We will be able to turn to God for things He can do to help us, instead of holding on to unrealistic expectations of Him which will never come about. The Bible, after all, repeatedly speaks of God as the special protector of the poor, the widow, and the orphan, without raising the question of how it happened that they became poor, widowed, or orphaned in the first place.

We can maintain our own self-respect and sense of goodness without having to feel that God has judged us and condemned us. We can be angry at what has happened to us, without feeling that we are angry at God. More than that, we can recognize our anger at life's unfairness, our instinctive compassion at seeing people suffer, as coming from God who teaches us to be angry at injustice and to feel compassion for the afflicted. Instead of feeling that we are opposed to God, we can feel that our indignation is God's anger at unfairness working through us, that when we cry out, we are still on God's side, and He is still on ours.

3

SOMETIMES
THERE IS
NO REASON

"IF the bad things that happen to us are the results of bad luck, and not the will of God," a woman asked me one evening after I had delivered a lecture on my theology, "what makes bad luck happen?" I was stumped for an answer. My instinctive response was that nothing makes bad luck happen; it just happens. But I suspected that there must be more to it than that.

This is perhaps the philosophical idea which is the key to everything else I am suggesting in this book. Can you accept the idea that some things happen for no reason, that there is randomness in the universe? Some people cannot handle that idea. They look for connections, striving desperately to make sense of all that happens. They convince themselves that God is cruel, or that they are sinners, rather than accept randomness. Sometimes, when they have made sense of ninety percent of everything they know, they let themselves assume that the other ten percent makes sense also, but lies beyond the reach of their understanding. But why do we have to insist on everything being reasonable? Why must everything happen for a specific reason? Why can't we let the universe have a few rough edges?

I can more or less understand why a man's mind might suddenly snap, so that he grabs a shotgun and runs out into the street, shooting at strangers. Perhaps he is an army veteran, haunted by memories of things he has seen and done in combat. Perhaps he has encountered more frustration and rejection than he can bear at home and at work. He has been treated like a "nonperson," someone who does not have to be taken seriously, until his rage boils over and he decides, "I'll show them that I matter after all."

To grab a gun and shoot at innocent people is irrational, unreasonable behavior, but I can understand it. What I cannot understand is why Mrs. Smith should be walking on that street at that moment, while Mrs. Brown chooses to step into a shop on a whim and saves her life. Why should Mr. Jones happen to be crossing the street, presenting a perfect target to the mad marksman, while Mr. Green, who never has more than one cup of coffee for breakfast, chooses to linger over a second cup that morning and is still indoors when the shooting starts? The lives of dozens of people will be affected by such trivial, unplanned decisions.

I understand that hot, dry weather, weeks without rain, increases the danger of forest fire, so that a spark, a match, or sunlight focused on a shard of glass, can set a forest ablaze. I understand that the course of that fire will be determined by, among other things, the direction in which the wind blows. But is there a sensible explanation for why wind and weather combine to direct a forest fire on a given day toward certain homes rather than others, trapping some people inside and sparing others? Or is it just a matter of pure luck?

When a man and a woman join in making love, the man's ejaculate swarms with tens of millions of sperm cells, each one carrying a slightly different set of biologically inherited characteristics. No moral intelligence decides which one of those teeming millions will fertilize a waiting egg. Some of the sperm cells will cause a child to be born with a physical handicap, perhaps a fatal malady. Others will give him not only good health, but superior athletic or musical ability, or creative intelligence. A child's life will be wholly shaped, the lives of parents and relatives will be deeply affected, by the random determination of that race.

Sometimes many more lives may be affected. Robert and Suzanne Massie, parents of a boy with hemophilia, did what most parents of afflicted children do. They read everything they could about their son's ailment. They learned that the only son of the last Czar of Russia was a hemophiliac, and in Robert's book *Nicholas and Alexandra*, he speculated on whether the child's illness, the result of the random mating of the "wrong" sperm with the "wrong" egg, might have distracted and upset the royal parents and affected their ability to govern, bringing on the Bolshevik Revolution. He suggested that Europe's most populous nation may have changed its form of government, affecting the lives of everyone in this century, because of that random genetic occurrence.

Some people will find the hand of God behind everything that happens. I visit a woman in the hospital whose car was run into by a drunken driver running a red light. Her vehicle was totally demolished, but miraculously she escaped with only two cracked ribs and a few superficial cuts from flying glass. She looks up at me from her hospital bed and says, "Now I know there is a God. If I could come out of that alive and in one piece, it must be because He is looking out for me up there." I smile and keep quiet, running the risk of letting her think that I agree with her (what rabbi would be opposed to belief in God?), because it is not the time or place for a theology seminar. But my mind goes back to a funeral I conducted two weeks earlier, for a young husband and father who died in a similar drunk-driver collision; and I remember another case, a child killed by a hit-and-run driver while roller-skating; and all the newspaper accounts of lives cut short in automobile accidents. The woman before me may believe that she is alive because God wanted her to survive, and I am not inclined to talk her out of it, but what would she or I say to those other families? That they were less worthy than she, less valuable in God's sight? That God wanted them to die at that particular time and manner, and did not choose to spare them?

Remember our discussion in chapter 1 of Thornton Wilder's *Bridge of San Luis Rey?* When five people fall to their deaths, Brother Juniper investigates and learns that each of the five had recently "put things together" in his life. He is tempted to conclude that the rope bridge's breaking was not an accident, but an aspect of God's providence. There are no accidents. But when laws of physics and metal fatigue cause a wing to fall off an airplane, or when human carelessness causes engine failure, so that a plane crashes, killing two hundred people, was it God's will that those two hundred should chance to be on a doomed plane that day? And if the two hundred and first passenger had a flat tire on the way to the airport and missed the flight, grumbling and cursing his luck as he saw the plane take off without him, was it God's will that he should live while the others died? If it were, I would have to wonder about what kind of message God was sending us with His apparently arbitrary acts of condemning and saving.

When Martin Luther King, Jr., was killed in April 1968, much was made of the fact that he had passed his peak as a black leader. Many alluded to the speech he gave the night before his death, in which he said that, like Moses, he had "been to the mountaintop and seen the Promised Land," implying that, like Moses, he would die before he reached it. Rather than accept his death as a senseless tragedy, many, like Wilder's Brother Juniper, saw evidence that God took Martin Luther King at just the right moment, to spare him the agony of living out his years as a "has-been," a rejected prophet. I could never accept that line of reasoning. I would like to think that God is concerned, not only with the ego of one black leader, but with the needs of tens of millions of black men, women, and children. It would be hard to explain in what way they were better off for Dr. King's having been murdered. Why can't we acknowledge that the assassination was an affront to God, even as it was to us, and a sidetracking of His purposes, rather than strain our imaginations to find evidence of God's fingerprints on the murder weapon?

Soldiers in combat fire their weapons at an anonymous, faceless enemy. They know that they cannot let themselves be distracted by thinking that the soldier on the other side may be a nice, decent person with a loving family and a promising career waiting at home. Soldiers understand that a speeding bullet has no conscience, that a falling mortar shell cannot discriminate between those whose death would be a tragedy and those who would never be missed. That is why soldiers develop a certain fatalism about their chances, speaking of the bullet with their name on it, of their number coming up, rather than calculating whether they *deserve* to die or not. That is why the Army will not send the sole surviving son of a bereaved family into combat, because the Army understands that it cannot rely on God to make things come out fairly, even as the Bible long ago ordered home from the army every man who had just betrothed a wife or built a new home, lest he die in battle and never come to enjoy them. The ancient Israelites, for all their profound faith in God, knew that they could not depend on God to impose a morally acceptable pattern on where the arrows landed.

Let us ask again: Is there always a reason, or do some things just happen at random, for no cause?

"In the beginning," the Bible tells us, "God created the heaven and the earth. The earth was formless and chaotic, with darkness covering everything." Then God began to work His creative magic on the chaos, sorting things out, imposing order where there had been randomness before. He separated the light from the darkness, the earth from the sky, the dry land from the sea. This is what it means to create: not to make something out of nothing, but to make order out of chaos. A creative scientist or historian does not make up facts but orders facts; he sees connections between them rather than seeing them as random data. A creative writer does not make up new words but arranges familiar words in patterns which say something fresh to us.

So it was with God, fashioning a world whose overriding principle was orderliness, predictability, in place of the chaos with which He started: regular sunrises and sunsets, regular tides, plants and animals that bore seeds inside them so that they could reproduce themselves, each after its own kind. By the end of the sixth day, God had finished the world He had set out to make, and on the seventh day He rested.

But suppose God didn't quite finish by closing time on the afternoon of the sixth day? We know today that the world took billions of years to take shape, not six days. The Creation story in Genesis is a very important one and has much to say to us, but its six-day time frame is not meant to be taken literally. Suppose that Creation, the process of replacing chaos with order, were still going on. What would that mean? In the biblical metaphor of the six days of Creation, we would find ourselves somewhere in the middle of Friday afternoon. Man was just created a few "hours" ago. The world is mostly an orderly, predictable place, showing ample evidence of God's thoroughness and handiwork, but pockets of chaos remain. Most of the time, the events of the universe follow firm natural laws. But every now and then, things happen not contrary to those laws of nature but outside them. Things happen which could just as easily have happened differently.

Even as I write this, the newscasts carry reports of a massive hurricane in the Carribean. Meteorologists are at a loss to predict whether it will spin out to sea or crash into populated areas of the Texas-Louisiana coastline. The biblical mind saw the earthquake that overthrew Sodom and Gomorrah as God's way of punishing the people of those cities for their depravities. Some medieval and Victorian thinkers saw the eruption of Vesuvius and the destruction of Pompeii as a way of putting an end to that society's immorality. Even today, the earthquakes in California are interpreted by some as God's way of expressing His displeasure with the alleged homosexual excesses of San Francisco or the heterosexual ones of Los Angeles. But most of us today see a hurricane, an earthquake, a volcano as having no conscience. I would not venture to predict the path of a hurricane on the basis of which communities deserve to be lashed and which ones to be spared.

A change of wind direction or the shifting of a tectonic plate can cause a hurricane or earthquake to move toward a populated area instead of out into an uninhabited stretch of land. Why? A random shift in weather patterns causes too much or too little rain over a farming area, and a year's harvest is destroyed. A drunken driver steers his car over the center line of the highway and collides with the green Chevrolet instead of the red Ford fifty feet farther away. An engine bolt breaks on flight 205 instead of on flight 209, inflicting tragedy on one random group of families rather than another. There is no message in all of that. There is no reason for those particular people to be afflicted rather than others. These events do not reflect God's choices. They happen at random, and randomness is another name for chaos, in those corners of the universe where God's creative light has not yet penetrated. And chaos is evil; not wrong, not malevolent, but evil nonetheless, because by causing tragedies at random, it prevents people from believing in God's goodness.

I once asked a friend of mine, an accomplished physicist, whether from a scientific perspective the world was becoming a more orderly place, whether randomness was increasing or decreasing with time. He replied by citing the second law of thermodynamics, the law of entropy: Every system left to itself will change in such a way as to approach equilibrium. He explained that this meant the world was changing in the direction of more randomness. Think of a group of marbles in a jar, carefully arranged by size and color. The more you shake the jar, the more that neat arrangement will give way to random distribution, until it will be only a coincidence to find one marble next to another of the same color. This, he said, is what is happening to the world. One hurricane might veer off to sea, sparing the coastal cities, but it would be a mistake to see any evidence of pattern or purpose to that. Over the course of time, some hurricanes will blow harmlessly out to sea, while others will head into populated areas and cause devastation. The longer you keep track of such things, the less of a pattern you will find.

I told him that I had been hoping for a different answer. I had hoped for a scientific equivalent of the first chapter of the Bible, telling me that with every passing "day" the realm of chaos was diminishing, and more of the universe was yielding to the rule of order. He told me that if it made me feel any better, Albert Einstein had the same problem. Einstein was uncomfortable with quantum physics and tried for years to disprove it, because it based itself on the hypothesis of things happening at random. Einstein preferred to believe that "God does not play dice with the cosmos."

It may be that Einstein and the Book of Genesis are right. A system *left to itself* may evolve in the direction of randomness. On the other hand, our world may not be a system left to itself. There may in fact be a creative impulse acting on it, the Spirit of God hovering over the dark waters, operating over the course of millennia to bring order out of the chaos. It may yet come to pass that, as "Friday afternoon" of the world's evolution ticks toward the Great Sabbath which is the End of Days, the impact of random evil will be diminished.

Or it may be that God finished His work of creating eons ago, and left the rest to us. Residual chaos, chance and mischance, things happening for no reason, will continue to be with us, the kind of evil that Milton Steinberg has called "the still unremoved scaffolding of the edifice of God's creativity." In that case, we will simply have to learn to live with it, sustained and comforted by the knowledge that the earthquake and the accident, like the murder and the robbery, are not the will of God, but represent that aspect of reality which stands independent of His will, and which angers and saddens God even as it angers and saddens us.

NO EXCEPTIONS
FOR
NICE PEOPLE

THE story is told of the youngster who came home from Sunday School, having been taught the biblical story of the crossing of the Red Sea. His mother asked him what he had learned in class, and he told her: "The Israelites got out of Egypt, but Pharoah and his army chased after them. They got to the Red Sea and they couldn't cross it. The Egyptian army was getting closer. So Moses got on his walkie-talkie, the Israeli air force bombed the Egyptians, and the Israeli navy built a pontoon bridge so the people could cross." The mother was shocked. "Is that the way they taught you the story?" "Well, no," the boy admitted, "but if I told it to you the way they told it to us, you'd never believe it."

Centuries ago, people found reassuring proof of God in stories of miracles. They would tell of how God divided the sea to let the Israelites cross on dry land. They would recount stories about God sending rain in answer to a righteous person's prayer, or about rivers reversing their courses and the sun moving backward in its flight. They would remember tales of Daniel emerging unhurt from the den of lions, and

Shadrach, Meshach, and Abednego surviving the fiery furnace. The point of all these stories was to prove that God cared about us so much that He was willing to suspend the laws of nature to support and protect those whom He favored.

But we today are like the little boy in the Sunday School story. We are told those stories and we are skeptical. If anything, we find proof of God precisely in the fact that laws of nature do not change. God has given us a wonderful, precise, orderly world. One of the things that makes the world livable is the fact that the laws of nature are precise and reliable, and always work the same way. There is gravity: heavy objects always fall toward the earth, so a builder can build a house without having his materials float away. There is chemistry: mixing certain elements in certain proportions always yields the same result, so a doctor can prescribe medication and know what will happen. We can predict when the sun will rise and set on any given day. We can even predict when the moon will block the sun for certain areas, causing an eclipse. To the ancients, an eclipse was an unnatural event which they interpreted as God's way of warning them. To us, it is a perfectly natural event, a reminder of how precise a universe God has given us.

Our human bodies are miracles, not because they defy laws of nature, but precisely because they obey them. Our digestive systems extract nutrients from food. Our skins help to regulate body temperature by perspiring. The pupils of our eyes expand and contract in response to light. Even when we get sick, our bodies have built-in defense mechanisms to fight the illness. All these wonderful things happen, usually without our being aware of them, in accordance with the most

57

precise laws of nature. That, not the legendary splitting of the Red Sea, is the real miracle.

But the unchanging character of these laws, which makes medicine and astronomy possible, also causes problems. Gravity makes objects fall. Sometimes they fall on people and hurt them. Sometimes gravity makes people fall off mountains and out of windows. Sometimes gravity makes people slip on ice or sink under water. We could not live without gravity, but that means we have to live with the dangers it causes.

Laws of nature treat everyone alike. They do not make exceptions for good people or for useful people. If a man enters a house where someone has a contagious disease, he runs the risk of catching that disease. It makes no difference why he is in the house. He may be a doctor or a burglar; disease germs cannot tell the difference. If Lee Harvey Oswald fires a bullet at President John Kennedy, laws of nature take over from the moment that bullet is fired. Neither the course of the bullet nor the seriousness of the wound will be affected by questions of whether or not President Kennedy was a good person, or whether the world would be better off with him alive or dead.

Laws of nature do not make exceptions for nice people. A bullet has no conscience; neither does a malignant tumor or an automobile gone out of control. That is why good people get sick and get hurt as much as anyone. No matter what stories we were taught about Daniel or Jonah in Sunday School, God does not reach down to interrupt the workings of laws of nature to protect the righteous from harm. This is a second area of our world which causes bad things to happen to good people, and God does not cause it and cannot stop it.

And really, how could we live in this world if He did? Let us suppose, for purposes of argument, that God was determined not to let anything bad happen to a good and pious person. If an Oswald shoots at the president, no matter how carefully he aims, God will make the bullet miss. If a wing falls off Air Force One, God will make it land safely. Would this be a better world, if certain people were immune to laws of nature because God favored them, while the rest of us had to fend for ourselves?

Let us suppose, again for purposes of argument, that I was one of those righteous people to whom God would not let anything bad happen, because I was an observant, charitable person with a young family, spending my life helping people. What would that mean? Would I be able to go out in my shirtsleeves in cold weather and not get sick, because God would prevent the workings of nature from doing me harm? Could I cross streets against the lights in the face of heavy traffic, and not be injured? Could I jump out of high windows when I was in too much of a hurry to wait for an elevator, and not hurt myself? A world in which good people suffer from the same natural dangers that others do causes problems. But a world in which good people were immune to those laws would cause even more problems.

Insurance companies refer to earthquakes, hurricanes, and other natural disasters as "acts of God." I consider that a case of using God's name in vain. I don't believe that an earthquake that kills thousands of innocent victims without reason is an act of God. It is an act of nature. Nature is morally blind, without values. It churns along, following its own laws, not caring who or what gets in the way. But God is not morally

blind. I could not worship Him if I thought He was. God stands for justice, for fairness, for compassion. For me, the earthquake is not an "act of God." The act of God is the courage of people to rebuild their lives after the earthquake, and the rush of others to help them in whatever way they can.

If a bridge collapses, if a dam breaks, if a wing falls off an airplane and people die, I cannot see that as God's doing. I cannot believe that God wanted all those people to die at that moment, or that He wanted some of them to die and had no choice but to condemn the others along with them. I believe that these calamities are all acts of nature, and that there is no moral reason for those particular victims to be singled out for punishment. Perhaps, as human beings apply their God-given intelligence to the area of natural disasters, we will one day be able to understand the physical processes behind earthquakes, hurricanes, and metal fatigue, and learn how to anticipate them or even prevent them. When that happens, fewer innocent people will fall victim to these so-called "acts of God."

I don't know why one person gets sick, and another does not, but I can only assume that some natural laws which we don't understand are at work. I cannot believe that God "sends" illness to a specific person for a specific reason. I don't believe in a God who has a weekly quota of malignant tumors to distribute, and consults His computer to find out who deserves one most or who could handle it best. "What did I do to deserve this?" is an understandable outcry from a sick and suffering person, but it is really the wrong question. Being sick or being healthy is not a matter of what God decides that we deserve. The better question is "if this has happened to

me, what do I do now, and who is there to help me do it?" As we saw in the previous chapter, it becomes much easier to take God seriously as the source of moral values if we don't hold Him responsible for all the unfair things that happen in the world.

But perhaps we ought to phrase our question differently. Instead of asking why good people have to suffer from the same laws of nature that bad people do, let us ask why any people have to suffer at all. Why do people have to get sick? Why do they have to feel pain? Why do people die? If God was designing a world for our maximum benefit, why could He not create unchanging laws of nature which would not do harm to any of us, good or bad?

> "Good God, how much reverence can you have for a Supreme Being who finds it necessary to include tooth decay in His divine system of creation? Why in the world did He ever create pain?"
> "Pain?" Lieutenant Shiesskopf's wife pounced upon the word victoriously. "Pain is a useful symptom. Pain is a warning to us of bodily dangers."
> "And who created the dangers?" Yossarian demanded. "Why couldn't He have used a doorbell to notify us, or one of His celestial choirs? Or a system of blue-and-red neon tubes right in the middle of each person's forehead?"
> "People would certainly look silly walking around with red neon tubes in the middle of their foreheads."
> "They certainly look beautiful now writhing in agony, don't they?" (Joseph Heller, *Catch-22*)

Why do we feel pain? Approximately one out of every 400,000 babies born is fated to live a short, pitiful life which

none of us would envy, a life in which he will frequently hurt himself, sometimes seriously, and not know it. That child has a rare genetic disease known as familial dysautonomia. He cannot feel pain. Such a child will cut himself, burn himself, fall down and break a bone, and never know that something is wrong. He will not complain of sore throats and stomach aches, and his parents will not know when he is sick until it is too late.

Would any of us want to live like that, without feeling pain? It is an unpleasant but necessary part of being alive. Author Joseph Heller may have his hero Yossarian make fun of the argument, but in fact pain *is* nature's way of telling us that we are overexerting ourselves, that some part of our body is not functioning as it was meant to, or is being asked to do more than it was intended to. Think of the stories you have read of athletes prematurely ending their careers, sometimes even crippling themselves permanently, because they forced themselves to ignore pain or took drugs that would stop the hurting without affecting the reason for it. Think of the people who had to be rushed to the hospital on an emergency basis, because they ignored the warning signs of mild pain, thinking it would go away if they did.

We feel pain when we strain our muscles beyond what they can take. We feel pain to make us jerk our hand away from something hot before it burns us seriously. We feel pain as a signal that something is wrong in that marvelously intricate machine, our body. We may mistakenly think of pain as one of God's ways of punishing us, perhaps remembering how one of our parents would slap us when we were children, perhaps believing that all unpleasant things that come our way

are punishments. In fact, the word "pain" comes from the same Latin root *poena* as do the words "punish" and "penalty." But pain does not represent God's punishing us. It represents nature's way of warning good and bad people alike that something is wrong. Life may be unpleasant because we are subject to pain. Someone has said that a man with a toothache walking through a forest can't appreciate the beauty of the forest because his tooth hurts him. But life would be dangerous, perhaps unlivable, if we could not feel pain.

But that sort of pain—the broken bone, the hot stove—is still a response at the animal level. Animals feel that sort of pain even as we do. You don't need to have a soul to feel pain when something sharp is stuck into your flesh. There is another level of pain, however, which only human beings can feel. Only human beings can find meaning in their pain.

Consider the following: scientists have found ways of measuring the intensity of the pain we feel. They can measure the fact that a migraine headache hurts more than a skinned knee. And they have determined that two of the most painful things human beings can experience are giving birth and passing a kidney stone. From a purely physical point of view, these two events both hurt equally, and hardly anything hurts more. But from a human point of view, the two are so different. The pain of passing a kidney stone is simply pointless suffering, the result of a natural malfunction somewhere in our body. But the pain of giving birth is creative pain. It is pain that has meaning, pain that gives life, that leads to something. That is why the person who passes a kidney stone will usually say "I'd give anything not to have to go through that again," but the woman who has given birth to a child, like the runner or mountain climber who has driven his body to reach a goal, can transcend her pain and contemplate repeating the experience.

Pain is the price we pay for being alive. Dead cells—our hair, our fingernails—can't feel pain; they cannot feel anything. When we understand that, our question will change from, "why do we have to feel pain?" to "what do we do with our pain so that it becomes meaningful and not just pointless empty suffering? How can we turn all the painful experiences of our lives into birth pangs or into growing pains?" We may not ever understand why we suffer or be able to control the forces that cause our suffering, but we can have a lot to say about what the suffering does to us, and what sort of people we become because of it. Pain makes some people bitter and envious. It makes others sensitive and compassionate. It is the result, not the cause, of pain that makes some experiences of pain meaningful and others empty and destructive.

Why did God create a world in which there is sickness and disease? I don't know why people get sick, sometimes fatally. I know that sicknesses are caused by germs and viruses (or at least, I take that on faith, never having seen a germ or a virus, but trusting my doctors to be honorable people who would not mislead me). I suspect that people get sick when they are depressed, when they feel rejected and can't look forward to the immediate future. I know that people recover from illness faster when they know that people care about them and when they have something to look forward to. But I don't have a good answer to the question of why our bodies had to be made vulnerable to germs and viruses and malignant tumors in the first place. I understand that the cells of which our bodies are made are constantly dying and being replaced. That makes it possible for us to grow bigger, and to grow new skin to replace scraped and bruised skin. I understand that when foreign presences invade our body, we mobilize our defenses to fight them, and the mobilization often causes our body temperature to rise and makes us feverish. I understand that for our bones to be flexible enough and light enough for us to be able to walk, they have to be fragile enough to break under severe strain. For a young man to be paralyzed because of a spinal cord injury in an accident which was not his fault is indescribably tragic, but at least it follows laws of nature which make sense.

As we have learned more about how the human body works, as we understand more of the natural laws built in to the world, we have some answers. We have come to understand that we cannot indefinitely abuse our bodies and neglect our health without increasing the risk of something going wrong. Our bodies are too sensitive; they have to be, to do the things we call on them to do. The man who smokes two packs of cigarettes a day for twenty years and develops lung cancer, faces problems which deserve our sympathy, but he has no grounds for asking, "How could God do this to me?" The person who weighs considerably more than he should, and whose heart has to pump blood through miles of additional fat cells and clogged arteries will have to pay the price for that additional strain on his system, and will have no grounds to complain to God. Neither, alas, will the doctor, the clergyman, or the politician who works long hours, seven-day week after seven-day week, in the noblest of causes, but fails to take care of his own health in the process.

But why cancer? Why blindness and diabetes and hypertension and kidney failure? Why do things spontaneously go wrong in our bodies without our having caused them through bad health habits? To explain that mental retardation results from a defective chromosome is to offer an explanation which does not really explain anything. Why should chromosomes become defective? And why should a person's potential for happiness in life depend on their not doing so?

I have no satisfying answer to those questions. The best answer I know is the reminder that Man today is only the latest stage in a long, slow evolutionary process. Once upon a time, the only living things in the world were plants. Then there were amphibian creatures; then came the higher, more complex animals, and finally Man. As life evolved from the simpler to the more complex, we retained and inherited some of the weaknesses of those earlier forms. Like plants, our bodies remain vulnerable to injury and decay. Like animals, we can grow sick and die. But there are no tragedies when plants die, and animals have one important advantage over humans. If something goes wrong in an animal's body, if something breaks down, leaving the animal weak and crippled, that animal is less likely to mate and to pass on its defective genes to the next generation. In that way, traits less suited to survival fade out, and the next generation is likely to be bigger, stronger, and healthier.

Human beings don't operate that way. A human being who is diabetic or has other inherited health problems, but is an attractive, sensitive person, will marry and have children. No one would deny him that right. But in the process, he will bring into the world children with a better-than-average chance of having something go wrong with their bodies.

Consider the following sequence of events. In the delivery room, a baby is born with a congenital heart defect or some other serious ailment hidden in his parents' genetic background which threatens his survival. If he were to die shortly after birth, his parents would go home, saddened but not overwhelmed by the tragedy. For a time they would be depressed, wondering about what might have been, but then they would begin to put it behind them and look to the future.

But the child does not die. Through the miracles of modern medicine and heroic devotion of nurses and doctors, he survives. He grows up, too frail to take part in sports, but bright and cheerful and popular. He becomes a doctor, or a teacher, or a poet. He marries and has children. He is respected in his profession and well-liked in his neighborhood. His family loves him; people learn to depend on him. Then, at age thirty-five or forty, his frail health catches up with him. His congenitally weak heart, which nearly failed him at birth, gives out and he dies. Now his death causes more than a few days of sadness. It is a shattering tragedy for his wife and children, and a profoundly saddening event for all the other people in his life.

We could prevent many tragedies like that one, if we were to let sickly children die at birth, if we worked less diligently to help them survive childhood illnesses and hazards, if we permitted only the healthiest specimens to marry and have children, and forbade others to know those satisfactions. After all, that is what animals do, so that genetic errors are not

67

passed on from generation to generation. But who among us, on moral grounds or simple self-interest, would agree to that?

Even as I write these lines, I think of a young man in my community who is slowly dying of a degenerative disease, and I find myself wondering if all this biological speculation will be of any consolation to him. I suspect that it will not. Unless we want to play the role of Job's comforters, why should we find it helpful to know that his illness follows certain natural laws? Will it make him feel any better to be told that his parents unknowingly passed on to him the seeds of his terrible illness?

Job asked questions about God, but he did not need lessons in theology. He needed sympathy and compassion and the reassurance that he was a good person and a cherished friend. My neighbor asks me questions about his illness, but we misunderstand his needs if we respond with lessons in biology and genetics. Like Job, he needs to be told that what is happening to him is dreadfully unfair. He needs help in keeping his mind and spirit strong, so that he can look forward to a future in which he will be able to think and plan and decide, even if he can't walk or swim, and will not have to become a helpless, dependent cripple even if he loses certain skills.

I don't know why my friend and neighbor is sick and dying and in constant pain. From my religious perspective, I cannot tell him that God has His reasons for sending him this terrible fate, or that God must specially love him or admire his bravery to test him in this way. I can only tell him that the God I believe in did not send the disease and does not have a miraculous cure that He is withholding. But in a world in which we all possess immortal spirits in fragile and vulnerable bodies, the God I believe in gives strength and courage to those who, unfairly and through no fault of their own, suffer pain and the fear of death. I can help him remember that he is more than a crippled body. He is more than a man with a debilitating illness. He is a man with a loving wife and children, with many friends, and with enough iron in his soul to remain a living person in the fullest sense of the word until the very last day.

I don't know why people are mortal and fated to die, and I don't know why people die at the time and in the way they do. Perhaps we can try to understand it by picturing what the world would be like if people lived forever.

When I was a freshman in college, I was a young man for whom old age and death were so remote that I never thought about them. But one of my freshman courses was in the classics of world literature, and I read two discussions of death and immortality which so impressed me that they have remained with me today, thirty years later.

In Homer's *Odyssey*, there is a passage in which Ulysses meets Calypso, a sea princess and a child of the gods. Calypso, a divine being, is immortal. She will never die. She is fascinated by Ulysses, never having met a mortal before. As we read on, we come to realize that Calypso envies Ulysses because he will not live forever. His life becomes more full of meaning, his every decision is more significant, precisely because his time is limited, and what he chooses to do with it represents a real choice.

Later that year I read Swift's *Gulliver's Travels*. In the land of the Luggnaggians, Swift writes in his fantasy, it happened once or twice in a generation that a child was born with a circular red spot in its forehead, signifying that it would never die. Gulliver imagines those children to be the most fortunate people imaginable, "being born exempt from that universal calamity of human nature," death. But as he comes to meet them, he realizes that they are in fact the most miserable and pitiable of creatures. They grow old and feeble. Their friends and contemporaries die off. At the age of eighty, their property is taken from them and given to their children, who would otherwise never inherit from them. Their bodies contract various ailments, they accumulate grudges and griev-ances, they grow weary of the struggle of life, and they can never look forward to being released from the pain of living.

Homer shows us an immortal being envying us for being mortal. Swift teaches us to pity the person who cannot die. He wants us to realize that living with the knowledge that we will die may be frightening and tragic, but knowing we will never die would be unbearable. We might wish for a longer life, or a happier one, but how could any of us endure a life that went on forever? For many of us, we will come to the point where death will be the only healer for the pain which our lives will have come to contain.

If people lived forever and never died, one of two things would have to happen. Either the world would become impossibly crowded, or else people would avoid having children to avoid that crowding. Humanity would be de-prived of that sense of a fresh start, that potential for something new under the sun, which the birth of a chi'd represents. In a world where people lived forever, we would probably never have been born.

But, as in our previous discussion of pain, we have to acknowledge that it is one thing to explain that mortality in general is good for people in general. It is something else again to try to tell someone who has lost a parent, a wife, or a child, that death is good. We don't dare try to do that. It would be cruel and thoughtless. All we can say to someone at a time like that is that vulnerability to death is one of the given conditions of life. We can't explain it any more than we can explain life itself. We can't control it, or sometimes even postpone it. All we can do is try to rise beyond the question "why did it happen?" and begin to ask the question "what do I do now that it has happened?"

~ 5

GOD LEAVES US
ROOM TO BE
HUMAN

ONE of the most important things that any religion can teach us is what it means to be human. The Bible's vision of Man is as fundamental to its overall outlook as its vision of God. Two passages at the very beginning of the Bible teach us about being human, and tell us how we, as human beings, relate to God and to the world around us.

The first is the statement in the opening chapter of the Book of Genesis that human beings are made in the image of God. At the climax of the Creation process, God is represented as saying, "Let us make Man in our image." Why the plural? Who is the "us," the "our" of which God speaks? My suggestion for understanding that sentence is to see it as connected to the sentence immediately before it, in which God creates animals. In a description of Creation which is astonishingly similar to the evolutionary process as scientists have come to unravel it, God first creates a world covered with water. He then causes the dry land to emerge, fills His world with plants, fish, birds, and reptiles, and finally with mammals. Having created the animals and beasts, He says *to them*: "Let us arrange for a new kind of creature to emerge, a human being, in *our* image, yours and Mine. Let us fashion a creature who will be like you, an animal, in some ways— needing to eat, to sleep, to mate—and will be like Me in other ways, rising above the animal level. You animals will contribute his physical dimension, and I will breathe a soul into him." And so, as the crown of Creation, human beings are created, part animal, part divine.

But what is the part of us that lifts us above the animal level, the part of ourselves that we share with God in a way that no other living creature does? For the answer to that question, we must turn to the second of the biblical passages, one of the most misunderstood stories in all of the Bible, the story of what happened in the Garden of Eden.

After God created Adam and Eve, we read, He set them in the garden and told them that they could eat the fruit of all the trees in the garden, including the Tree of Life. Only the Tree of the Knowledge of Good and Evil was forbidden to them. God warned them that on the day they ate of that tree, they would die. Partly because of the serpent's urging, they ate the forbidden fruit. God confronted them with their disobedience and punished them in the following ways:

—They must leave the garden and no longer eat the fruit of the Tree of Life. (They do not die that day, but are told that they will now bear children and die, instead of living forever.)
—Eve will find the process of bearing and raising children painful. ("I will greatly multiply your pain and anguish; in pain will you bring forth children.")

73

—Adam will have to work to grow food instead of merely finding it on trees. ("By the sweat of your brow will you earn your bread.")
—There will be sexual tension between men and women. ("Your desire will be for your husband, but he will rule over you.")

When you first read that story, or when it was first taught to you in Sunday School, you probably understood it as a simple story of Adam and Eve disobeying God's command and being punished for it. That was an appropriate level for a child to respond at, and certainly a familiar message. ("Mommy told you not to play in the mud. You played in the mud anyway. Now you get no dessert.") Perhaps, depending on the religious tradition in which you were raised, you were told that all human beings, Adam's and Eve's descendants, were doomed to die as sinners because of that original disobedience. Maybe even then you felt that it was unfair for God to punish them and their descendants so severely for one little mistake committed by a couple of inexperienced people, especially if they could not have been expected to know what good and evil were before they ate from the Tree of Knowledge of Good and Evil.

I think there is more to the story than a simple case of disobeying God and being punished for it. My interpretation may be very different from the ones you have grown up with, but I think it makes sense and fits the biblical context. I think the story is about the differences between being human and being an animal, and the key to understanding it is the fact that the "forbidden" tree is called the Tree of the Knowledge of Good and Evil.

Human beings live in a world of good and bad, and that makes our lives painful and complicated. Animals don't; their lives are much simpler, without the moral problems and moral decisions that we humans have to face. Categories of "good" and "bad" don't really exist for animals. They can be helpful or messy, obedient or disobedient, but they can't be good or bad. Terms like "good doggie" or "bad doggie" don't refer to the moral value of what the dog chooses to do, but only to its being convenient or inconvenient for us, like "good weather" and "bad weather." Like our almost-but-not-quite-human ancestors, animals eat from the Tree of Life; they eat and drink, they run and they mate. But the Tree of Knowledge of Good and Evil is off limits to them.

To use a term which no one before our generation could have understood, animals are "programmed." Built-in instincts tell them when to eat, when to sleep, and so on. They follow their instincts and have very few difficult decisions to make. Human beings, however, are unique in the world of living creatures. The "image of God" in us permits us to say No to instinct on moral grounds. We can choose not to eat even though we are hungry. We can refrain from sex even when our instincts are aroused, not because we are afraid of being punished, but because we understand the terms "good" and "bad" in a way that no other animal can. The whole story of being human is the story of rising above our animal nature, and learning to control our instincts.

Let us look again at the "punishments" God visits on Adam

and Eve. (I put the word "punishments" in quotation marks because I am not sure they are really punishments. They are the painful consequences of being human rather than being a mere animal.) Every one of them represents a way in which life is more painful and problematic for human beings than it is for animals.

Sex and reproduction are natural and nonproblematic for all animals except Man. Females come into heat, males are attracted to them, and the species is maintained. Nothing could be simpler. Compare that to the sexual tensions existing among human beings: the teenage girl who waits for a boy to call her, feeling shunned and unattractive; the college student who cannot concentrate on his studies and is contemplating suicide because his girlfriend has broken up with him; the pregnant unmarried career woman who does not believe in abortion but is not sure what other choice she has; the severely depressed housewife whose husband has left her for another woman; the victims of rape, the patrons of pornographic movies, the furtive adulterers, the self-hating promiscuous "sexual athletes." Sex is so simple and straightforward for animals, and so painful for the rest of us (unless we are willing to behave like animals), because we have entered the world of good and evil.

But at the same time, precisely because we live in that world, a sexual relationship can mean infinitely more to us than it can to an animal, or to a person who sees sex only as an instinct to be satisfied. It can mean tenderness, sharing of affection, responsible commitment. Animals can mate and reproduce, but only human beings can know love, with all the pain that love sometimes involves.

For animals, giving birth to young and supervising their growing up is a purely instinctive process. There is much less physical pain, and much less psychological pain, involved for them than there is for the human parent. When our family dog had a litter of puppies, she knew exactly what to do without ever being told. Giving birth was uncomfortable, but not as painful as for a human mother. Our dog nursed her litter of puppies, and when they were old enough to take care of themselves, she began to ignore them. Now, when she meets one of her grown children, she recognizes another dog, but not necessarily one she is closely related to. Being a human parent can never be that easy. Giving birth, one of the most painful events a human body can experience, is in a sense the easiest part. Raising and teaching children, passing your values on to them, sharing their big and little hurts, being disappointed in them, knowing when to be tough and when to be forgiving—these are the painful parts of being a parent. And unlike the animals, we can't do it on instinct alone. We have to make hard choices.

Similarly, people have to work hard for their food, either growing it themselves or performing some service to earn money to buy it. The world provides food for animals, for those who hunt and for those who graze. A lion may have to exert himself to stalk and kill an animal, and it may be very hard for him, but it cannot compare to the human experience of being fired from a job or having to decide whether to withhold important information when making a sale. Animals can depend on instinct to guide them in their search for food. Only humans in their work have to worry about choosing a career, keeping a job, getting along with the boss. Only humans have to weigh the pros and cons of doing something that may be illegal or unethical to keep a job or make a sale. Once again, a major area of life which may be difficult for animals but is at least free of moral dilemmas, is for human beings a problematic and often painful area.

And finally, all living creatures are fated to die, but only human beings know it. Animals will instinctively protect themselves against threats to their life and well-being, but only human beings live in the valley of the shadow of death, with the knowledge that they are mortal, even when no one is attacking them. This knowledge that we are going to die someday changes our lives in many ways. It moves us to try to cheat death by doing something that will outlive us—having children, writing books, having an impact on our friends and neighbors so that they will remember us fondly. Knowing that our time is limited gives value to the things we do. It matters that we choose to read a book or visit a sick friend instead of going to the movies, precisely because we don't have the time to do everything.

This, then, is what happened to Adam and Eve. They became human. They had to leave the Garden of Eden, where animals eat from the Tree of Life, the tree of basic life-forces and instincts. They entered the world of the knowledge of good and evil, a more painful, more complicated world, where they would have to make difficult moral choices. Eating and working, having children and raising children would no longer be simple matters, as they are for lower animals. These first human beings were now self-conscious (after eating the forbidden fruit, they felt the need to put on clothes). They knew that they would not live forever. But most of all, they would have to spend their lives making choices.

This is what it means to be human "in the image of God." It means being free to make choices instead of doing whatever our instincts would tell us to do. It means knowing that some choices are good, and others are bad, and it is our job to know the difference. "Behold, I have set before you the path of good and the path of evil, the way of life and the way of death. Choose Life." (Deuteronomy 30:19) That could not be said to any other living creature except Man, for no other creature is free to choose.

But if Man is truly free to choose, if he can show himself as being virtuous by freely choosing the good when the bad is equally possible, then he has to be free to choose the bad also. If he were only free to do good, he would not really be choosing. If we are *bound* to do good, then we are not free to *choose* it.

Imagine a parent saying to a child, "How would you like to spend this afternoon, doing homework or playing with a friend? You choose." The child says, "I'd like to play with my friend." The parent responds, "I'm sorry, that's the wrong choice. I can't let you do that. I won't let you out of the house until your homework gets done. Choose again." This time the child says, "All right, I'll do my homework." The parent smiles and says, "I'm glad you made the right choice." We may have ended up with the preferred result, but it would be wrong to say that it was the child who showed maturity and responsibility by making that choice.

Now imagine God saying to a person, "How do you plan to

79

get the money to pay your bills? Are you going to get a job, which means getting up early in the morning and doing hard work, or are you going to grab an old lady's pocketbook and run off with it?" The man answers, "I was thinking of going out and stealing a pocketbook." God says, "No, that's wrong. I won't let you do that. Choose again." This time the man reluctantly agrees to get a job. A robbery has been prevented, but has the man been permitted to operate as a morally free human being? Has God permitted him to choose between the path of good and the path of evil? Or has God reduced him to the level of an animal by taking away his freedom to choose, and compelling him to take the better path?

In order to let us be free, in order to let us be human, God has to leave us free to choose to do right or to do wrong. If we are not free to choose evil, then we are not free to *choose* good either. Like the animals, we can only be convenient or inconvenient, obedient or disobedient. We can no longer be moral, which means we can no longer be human.

None of us can read God's mind, to know why, at a certain point in the evolutionary process, He had a new kind of creature emerge, a morally free animal who could choose to be good or bad. But He did, and the world has seen a lot of nobility and a lot of cruelty ever since.

Our moral freedom means that, if we choose to be selfish or dishonest, we can *be* selfish and dishonest, and God will not stop us. If we want to take something that does not belong to us, God will not reach down and pull our hand away from the cookie jar. If we want to hurt someone, God will not intervene to keep us from doing it. All He will do is tell us that certain things are wrong, warn us that we will be sorry for having done them, and hope that, if we don't take His word for it, we will at least learn from experience.

God is not like a human parent who watches as his child takes its first shaky steps or struggles with an algebra assignment, and who says to himself, "If I intervene, I will spare my child a lot of pain, but how will he ever learn to do it for himself?" A human parent in that situation has the possibility (and the responsibility) to intervene if the child is on the verge of doing himself serious harm. But God has set Himself the limit that He will not intervene to take away our freedom, including our freedom to hurt ourselves and others around us. He has already let Man evolve morally free, and there is no turning back the evolutionary clock.

Why, then, do bad things happen to good people? One reason is that our being human leaves us free to hurt each other, and God can't stop us without taking away the freedom that makes us human. Human beings can cheat each other, rob each other, hurt each other, and God can only look down in pity and compassion at how little we have learned over the ages about how human beings should behave. This line of reasoning helps me understand that monstrous eruption of evil we speak of as the Holocaust, the death of millions of innocent people at the hands of Adolf Hitler. When people ask, "Where was God in Auschwitz? How could He have permitted the Nazis to kill so many innocent men, women, and children?", my response is that it was not God who caused it. It was caused by human beings choosing to be cruel to their fellow men. In the words of a German Christian theologian, Dorothee Soelle, speaking of attempts to justify the Holocaust as God's will, "Who wants such a God? Who gains anything from worshipping Him? Was God on the side of the victims or on the side of the executioner?"

To try to explain the Holocaust, or any suffering, as God's will is to side with the executioner rather than with his victim, and to claim that God does the same.

I cannot make sense of the Holocaust by taking it to be God's will. Even if I could accept the death of an innocent individual now and then without having to rethink all of my beliefs, the Holocaust represents too many deaths, too much evidence against the view that "God is in charge and He has His reasons." I have to believe that the Holocaust was at least as much of an offense to God's moral order as it is to mine, or how can I respect God as a source of moral guidance?

Why did six million Jews, and several million other innocent victims, die in Hitler's death camps? Who was responsible? We fall back on the idea of human freedom to choose. Man, we discovered, is that unique creature whose behavior is not "programmed." He is free to choose to be good, which means he must be free to choose to be evil. Some good people are good on a relatively modest scale. They are charitable, they visit the sick, they help a neighbor change a flat tire. Others are good on a grander scale. They work diligently to discover a cure for a disease, or they fight for the extension of the rights of the poor and the powerless. Some bad people choose evil, but have the capacity to be evil only on a small scale. They lie, cheat, take things that do not belong to them. And some have the ability to do harm to millions, even as their good counterparts have the ability to be helpful to millions.

Hitler must have been one of those rare geniuses of evil who, having chosen to be destructive, had the ability to be more destructive than virtually anyone else in history. (This raises a question which is not really part of our discussion: Can we say that someone like Hitler *chose* to be destructive? Or would we have to go back and look at his parents, his home environment, his teachers, his early life experiences and historical circumstances that made him become the person he was? There is probably no clear answer to that question. Social scientists have been debating it for years, and will continue to do so. I can only say that the cornerstone of my religious outlook is the belief that human beings *are* free to choose the direction their life will take. Granted, some children are born with physical or mental capacities which limit their freedom of choice. Not everyone can choose to be an opera singer, a surgeon, or a professional athlete. Granted further that some parents mishandle their children badly, that accidental events—wars, illnesses—traumatize children so badly that they may not be able to do something they would otherwise be qualified for, and that some people are so addicted to habits that it is hard to speak of them as being free. But I will insist that every adult, no matter how unfortunate a childhood he had or how habit-ridden he may be, is free to make choices about his life. If we are not free, if we are bound by circumstances and experiences, then we are no different from the animal who is bound by instinct. To say of Hitler, to say of any criminal, that he did not choose to be bad but was a victim of his upbringing, is to make all morality, all discussion of right and wrong, impossible. It leaves unanswered the question of why people in similar circumstances did not all become Hitlers. But worse, to say "it is not his fault, he was not free to choose" is to rob a person of his humanity, and reduce him to the level of an animal who is similarly not free to choose between right and wrong.

The Holocaust happened because Hitler was a demented evil genius who chose to do harm on a massive scale. But he did not cause it alone. Hitler was only one man, and even his ability to do evil was limited. The Holocaust happened because thousands of others could be persuaded to join him in his madness, and millions of others permitted themselves to be frightened or shamed into cooperating. It happened because angry, frustrated people were willing to vent their anger and frustration on innocent victims as soon as someone encouraged them to do so. It happened because Hitler was able to persuade lawyers to forget their commitment to justice and doctors to violate their oaths. And it happened because democratic governments were unwilling to summon their people to stand up to Hitler as long as their own interests were not yet at stake.

Where was God while all this was going on? Why did He not intervene to stop it? Why didn't He strike Hitler dead in 1939 and spare millions of lives and untold suffering, or why didn't He send an earthquake to demolish the gas chambers? Where was God? I have to believe, with Dorothee Soelle, that He was with the victims, and not with the murderers, but that He does not control man's choosing between good and evil. I have to believe that the tears and prayers of the victims aroused God's compassion, but having given Man freedom to choose, including the freedom to choose to hurt his neighbor, there was nothing God could do to prevent it.

Christianity introduced the world to the idea of a God who suffers, alongside the image of a God who creates and commands. Postbiblical Judaism also occasionally spoke of a God who suffers, a God who is made homeless and goes into exile along with His exiled people, a God who weeps when He sees what some of His children are doing to others of His children. I don't know what it means for God to suffer. I don't believe that God is a person like me, with real eyes and real tear ducts to cry, and real nerve endings to feel pain. But I would like to think that the anguish I feel when I read of the sufferings of innocent people reflects God's anguish and God's compassion, even if His way of feeling pain is different from ours. I would like to think that He is the source of my being able to feel sympathy and outrage, and that He and I are on the same side when we stand with the victim against those who would hurt him.

The last word, appropriately, comes from a survivor of Auschwitz:

It never occurred to me to question God's doings or lack of doings while I was an inmate of Auschwitz, although of course I understand others did. . . . I was no less or no more religious because of what the Nazis did to us; and I believe my faith in God was not undermined in the least. It never occurred to me to associate the calamity we were experiencing with God, to blame Him, or to believe in Him less or cease believing in Him at all because He didn't come to our aid. God doesn't owe us that, or anything. We owe our lives to Him. If someone believes God is responsible for the death of six million because He didn't somehow do something to save them, he's got his thinking reversed. We owe God our lives for the few or many years we live, and we have the duty to worship Him and do as He commands us. That's what we're here on earth for, to be in God's service, to do God's bidding.

(Brenner, *The Faith and Doubt of Holocaust Survivors*)

6

GOD HELPS THOSE WHO STOP HURTING THEMSELVES

ONE of the worst things that happens to a person who has been hurt by life is that he tends to compound the damage by hurting himself a second time. Not only is he the victim of rejection, bereavement, injury, or bad luck; he often feels the need to see himself as a bad person who had this coming to him, and because of that drives away people who try to come close to him and help him. Too often, in our pain and confusion, we instinctively do the wrong thing. We don't feel we deserve to be helped, so we let guilt, anger, jealousy, and self-imposed loneliness make a bad situation even worse.

I once read of an Iranian folk proverb, "If you see a blind man, kick him; why should you be kinder than God?" In other words, if you see someone who is suffering, you must believe that he deserves his fate and that God wants him to suffer. Therefore, put yourself on God's side by shunning him or humiliating him further. If you try to help him, you will be going against God's justice.

Most of us probably respond to this point of view with the feeling, "That's terrible." We usually think that we know better than to do that. But too often we inadvertently find ourselves saying to people who have been hurt that they, in some way, deserved it. And when we do that, we feed into their latent sense of guilt, the suspicion that maybe this happened to them because they did somehow have it coming.

Do you remember Job's comforters from the biblical story? When the three friends came to visit Job, they genuinely wanted to comfort him for his losses and his illness. But they did almost everything wrong, and ended up by making him feel worse. Can we learn from their mistakes what a person needs when he has been hurt by life, and how we as friends and neighbors can be helpful to him?

Their first mistake was to think that when Job said, "Why is God doing this to me?" he was asking a question, and that they would be helping him by answering his question, by explaining why God was doing it. In reality, Job's words were not a theological question at all, but a cry of pain. There should have been an exclamation point after those words, not a question mark. What Job needed from his friends—what he was really asking for when he said "Why is God doing this to me?"—was not theology, but sympathy. He did not really want them to explain God to him, and he certainly did not want them to show him where his theology was faulty. He wanted them to tell him that he was in fact a good person, and that the things that were happening to him were terribly tragic and unfair. But the friends got so bogged down talking about God that they almost forgot about Job, except to tell him that he must have done something pretty awful to deserve this fate at the hands of a righteous God.

Because the friends had never been in Job's position, they

could not realize how unhelpful, how offensive it was for them to be judging Job, to be telling him he should not cry and complain so much. Even if they themselves had experienced similar losses, they would still have no right to sit in judgment of Job's grief. It is hard to know what to say to a person who has been struck by tragedy, but it is easier to know what not to say. Anything critical of the mourner ("don't take it so hard," "try to hold back your tears, you're upsetting people") is wrong. Anything which tries to minimize the mourner's pain ("it's probably for the best," "it could be a lot worse," "she's better off now") is likely to be misguided and unappreciated. Anything which asks the mourner to disguise or reject his feelings ("we have no right to question God," "God must love you to have selected you for this burden") is wrong as well.

Under the impact of his multiple tragedies, Job was trying desperately to hold on to his self-respect, his sense of himself as a good person. The last thing in the world he needed was to be told that what he was doing was wrong. Whether the criticisms were about the way he was grieving or about what he had done to deserve such a fate, their effect was that of rubbing salt into an open wound.

Job needed sympathy more than he needed advice, even good and correct advice. There would be a time and place for that later. He needed compassion, the sense that others felt his pain with him, more than he needed learned theological explanations about God's ways. He needed physical comforting, people sharing their strength with him, holding him rather than scolding him.

He needed friends who would permit him to be angry, to

cry and to scream, much more than he needed friends who would urge him to be an example of patience and piety to others. He needed people to say, "Yes, what happened to you is terrible and makes no sense," not people who would say, "Cheer up, Job, it's not all that bad." And that was where his friends let him down. The phrase "Job's comforters" has come into the language to describe people who mean to help, but who are more concerned with their own needs and feelings than they are with those of the other person, and so end up only making things worse.

Job's friends did do at least two things right, though. First of all, they came. I am sure that the prospect of seeing their friend in his misery was painful for them to contemplate, and they must have been tempted to stay away and leave him alone. It is not pleasant to see a friend suffering, and most of us would rather avoid the experience. We either stay away entirely, so that the suffering person experiences isolation and a sense of rejection on top of his tragedy, or we come and try to avoid the reason for our being there. Hospital visits and condolence calls become discussions of the weather, the stock market, or the pennant race, taking on an air of unreality as the most important subject on the mind of everyone present is left conspicuously unmentioned. Job's friends at least mustered the courage to face him and to confront his sorrow.

And secondly, they listened. According to the biblical account, they sat with Job for several days, not saying anything, while Job poured out his grief and anger. That, I suspect, was the most helpful part of their visit. Nothing they did after that did Job as much good. When Job finished his outburst, they should have said, "Yes, it's really awful. We don't know how you put up with it," instead of feeling compelled to defend God and conventional wisdom. Their silent presence must have been a lot more helpful to their friend than their lengthy theological explanations were. We can all learn a lesson from that.

I had an experience some years ago which taught me something about the ways in which people make a bad situation worse by blaming themselves. One January, I had to officiate at two funerals on successive days for two elderly women in my community. Both had died "full of years," as the Bible would say; both succumbed to the normal wearing out of the body after a long and full life. Their homes happened to be near each other, so I paid condolence calls on the two families on the same afternoon.

At the first home, the son of the deceased woman said to me, "If only I had sent my mother to Florida and gotten her out of this cold and snow, she would be alive today. It's my fault that she died." At the second home, the son of the other deceased woman said, "If only I hadn't insisted on my mother's going to Florida, she would be alive today. That long airplane ride, the abrupt change of climate, was more than she could take. It's my fault that she's dead."

When things don't turn out as we would like them to, it is very tempting to assume that had we done things differently, the story would have had a happier ending. Clergymen know that any time there is a death, the survivors will feel guilty. Because the course of action they took turned out badly, they believe that the opposite course—keeping Mother at home, deferring the operation—would have turned out better. After all, how could it have turned out any worse? Survivors feel guilty for still being alive while a loved one is dead. They feel guilty when they think of all the kind words they never got around to saying to the deceased, and the good things they never found time to do for her. Indeed, many of the mourning rituals in all religions are designed to help the bereaved get rid of these irrational feelings of guilt for a tragedy they did not in fact cause. But the sense of guilt, the sense of "it's my fault," seems to be universal.

There seem to be two elements involved in our readiness to feel guilt. The first is our strenuous need to believe that the world makes sense, that there is a cause for every effect and a reason for everything that happens. That leads us to find patterns and connections both where they really exist (smoking leads to lung cancer; people who wash their hands have fewer contagious diseases) and where they exist only in our minds (the Red Sox win every time I wear my lucky sweater; that boy I like talks to me on odd-numbered days, but not on even-numbered ones, except where there has been a holiday to throw the pattern off.) How many public and personal superstitions are based on something good or bad having happened right after we did something, and our assuming that the same thing will follow the same pattern every time?

The second element is the notion that *we* are the cause of what happens, especially the bad things that happen. It seems to be a short step from believing that every event has a cause to believing that every disaster is our fault. The roots of this feeling may lie in our childhood. Psychologists speak of the infantile myth of omnipotence. A baby comes to think that the world exists to meet his needs, and that he makes everything happen in it. He wakes up in the morning and summons the rest of the world to its tasks. He cries, and someone comes to attend to him. When he is hungry, people feed him, and when he is wet, people change him. Very often, we do not completely outgrow that infantile notion that our wishes cause things to happen. A part of our mind continues to believe that people get sick because we hate them.

Our parents, in fact, often feed this notion. Not realizing how vulnerable our childhood egos are, they snap at us when they are tired or frustrated for reasons that have nothing to do with us. They bawl us out for being in the way, for leaving toys around or having the television set on too loud, and we in our childhood innocence assume that they are justified and we are the problem. Their anger may pass in a moment, but we continue to bear the scars of feeling at fault, thinking that whenever something goes wrong, we are to blame for it. Years later, should something bad happen to us or around us, feelings from our childhood reemerge and we instinctively assume that we have messed things up again.

Even Job would rather have had God document his guilt than admit that it was all a mistake. If he could be shown that he deserved his fate, then at least the world would make sense. It would be no pleasure to suffer for one's misdeeds, but it might be easier to take than finding out that we live in a random world where things happen for no reason.

Sometimes, of course, a feeling of guilt is appropriate and necessary. Sometimes we *have* caused the sorrow in our lives and ought to take responsibility. The man who sat in my office one day, telling me how he left his wife and young children to marry his secretary, and asking me how I could help him get over his guilt for what he had done to his children, was making an improper request of me. He *should* have felt guilty, and he should have been thinking in terms of making amends to his first family rather than looking for a way to shake his sense of guilt. A sense of our inadequacies and failings, a recognition that we could be better people than we usually are, is one of the forces for moral growth and improvement in our society. An appropriate sense of guilt makes people try to be better. But an excessive sense of guilt, a tendency to blame ourselves for things which are clearly not our fault, robs us of our self-esteem and perhaps of our capacity to grow and to act.

One of the hardest things Bob ever did was to put his seventy-eight-year-old mother in a nursing home. It was a borderline case, because his mother was basically alert and healthy and did not require medical care, but could no longer feed or take care of herself. Six months earlier, Bob and his wife had taken her into their home after her apartment caught fire when she forgot to turn off the stove. She was lonely, depressed, and confused. Bob's wife had to come home from her job at noon to give her mother-in-law lunch and sit her in front of the television set until the children came home from school. Bob's teenage daughter cut down on her evening social life to "baby-sit" for Grandma when Bob and his wife went out. The children were discouraged from bringing friends into the house: "It's a small house and gets awfully noisy." After a few weeks, it was clear that the arrangement was not working out. The members of the family were becoming edgy and irritable with one another. Each one was keeping score of how much he or she had "given up." Bob loved his mother, the children loved Grandma, but they realized that she needed more than they were in a position to give. They were not prepared to make the sacrifices of time and life-style which caring for a sick old woman required. They talked it over one night, made some inquiries, and reluctantly, but with a palpable sense of relief, placed her in a nearby nursing home. Bob knew that he was doing the right thing, but he still felt guilty about it. His mother hadn't wanted to go. She offered to be less demanding at home, to be less in the way. She cried when she saw the older, more crippled residents of the home, wondering perhaps how soon she would come to look like them.

That weekend, Bob, who did not usually think of himself as a religious person, decided to go to services before he drove out to visit his mother. He was feeling strange about the visit, afraid of what he would find or what his mother would tell him, and he hoped that going to a religious service would give him the tranquillity and peace of mind he needed. As luck would have it, the sermon that morning was on the Fifth Commandment, "Honor your father and mother." The clergyman spoke of the sacrifices parents make in raising children, and of the reluctance of children to appreciate those sacrifices. He criticized the self-centeredness of today's younger generation, saying, "Why is it that one mother can care for six children, but six children can't care for one mother?" All around Bob were older men and women, nodding their heads approvingly.

Bob left the service feeling hurt and angry. He felt that he had just been told, in the name of God, that he was a selfish and uncaring person. At lunch, he was irritable with his wife and children. At the nursing home, he was impatient with his mother and unable to respond to her. He was ashamed of what he had done to her, and angry at her for being the cause of his embarrassment and condemnation. The visit was an emotional disaster, leaving all parties wondering if the placement would ever work out. Bob was haunted by the idea that his mother didn't have long to live, and that when she died, he would never be able to forgive himself for having made her last years miserable because of his selfishness.

Bob's situation would have been difficult under any circumstances. The guilt feelings, the ambivalence were there from the start. The helplessness of aging parents, their appeals to their children, tap feelings of inadequacy, buried resentment, and guilt in many perfectly decent people. It is a hard situation to handle under the best of conditions. The parents are often scared, vulnerable, and sometimes emotionally immature as well. They may not be above using illness, loneliness, or guilt to manipulate their children into giving them the attention they desperately need. The proverbial Jewish mother who keeps reminding her children of her sacrifices in the name of their happiness, creating a debt that no one could work off in a lifetime, has become a stock figure of literature and humor. (How many Jewish mothers does it take to change a light bulb? None; "Don't worry about me. Go have a good time. I'll be all right sitting here in the dark.") But Bob's situation was made worse by his hearing the voice of religion as a judgmental one. There should be sermons about the honor due parents, but they should be careful not to play upon people's predisposition to feel guilty. Had Bob been more clearheaded that morning, he might have told the preacher that perhaps six children can't take care of one mother because those six children all have spouses and children of their own. He could have explained that he loved his mother, but had a primary loyalty to the well-being of his own wife and children, even as, when he was young, his mother had loved her parents but had been more concerned with him than she was with them. Had Bob been more confident of the rightness of what he had done, he might have spoken back to those accusations. But because he walked into the service feeling just a little guilty, the minister's words seemed to confirm his own troubling thoughts that he was, in fact, a bad and selfish person.

Our egos are so vulnerable, it is so easy to make us feel that we are bad people, that it is unworthy of religion to manipulate us in that way. Indeed, the goal of religion should be to help us feel good about ourselves when we have made honest and reasonable, but sometimes painful choices about our lives.

Even more than adults, children tend to see themselves as the center of their world, and to believe that their acts make things happen. They need a lot of reassurance that when a parent dies, they did not cause it. "Daddy didn't die because you were angry at him. He died because he had an accident (or a serious sickness) and all the doctors couldn't make him get better. We know that you loved your daddy, even if sometimes you got angry at him. We all get angry at people we love sometimes, but that doesn't mean that we don't love them or that we really want something bad to happen to them."

Children need to be assured that the parent who died did not reject them or *choose* to leave them, an idea they might easily get from such explanations as "Daddy's gone away and he won't be coming back." Even the author of the Twenty-seventh Psalm in the Bible, a mature adult and a gifted poet, speaks of the death of his parents in those terms: "For my father and mother have left me." He is so emotionally involved in their deaths that he cannot see things from their point of view, that they were sick and died, but only from his own, that *they* left *him*. It would be good to reassure a child that her father wanted to live, that he wanted to come home from the hospital and do things with her the way he used to, but the illness or accident was so bad that he couldn't.

To try to make a child feel better by telling him how beautiful it is in heaven and how happy his father is to be with God is another way of depriving him of the chance to grieve. When we do that, we ask a child to deny and mistrust his own feelings, to be happy when he really wants to be sad even as all of us around him are sad.

The child's right to feel upset and angry, and the appropriateness of her being angry at the situation (not at the deceased parent or at God) should be recognized at a time like this.

The death of another child, whether brother, friend, or stranger whose death is publicized in the media, also introduces into the child's world a sense of vulnerability. For the first time, he realizes that something scary and painful can happen to someone his age. I had been in my present congregation less than a year when I was called on to break the news to a father and mother that their five-year-old son had been run over and killed by the bus that was bringing him home from day camp. In addition to trying to help the parents deal with their own overwhelming grief (and in addition to dealing with my own feelings—I liked the boy, I liked the family, and I had recently learned that my own son would die young), I had to explain to my own children and to other youngsters in the community how such a thing could happen to a young child.

(As I was leaving to be with the parents the evening after the accident, my son Aaron, who was then four, asked me where I was going. I was reluctant to tell him that a boy nearly his own age had been killed, and then run out of the house before we could talk about it, so I said that a boy had been hurt in an accident and I was going to see how he was doing. At seven the next morning, Aaron's first words to me were, "Is the little boy all right?")

My answer to the dead child's neighborhood and nursery school playmates came in two parts. First, I told them that what had happened to Jonathan was very unusual. That was why everybody was talking about it. That was why it was on the radio and the front page of the local newspaper. This sort of thing so rarely happens that it is big news when it does, because it is so unusual. Almost all the time, children get off buses and cross streets safely. Almost all the time, children who fall down and hurt themselves get better after a little while. Almost all the time, when children get sick, doctors are able to make them feel better. But sometimes, on very rare occasions, a child gets hurt or gets sick and nobody can make him better, and he dies. When that happens, everybody is very surprised and very sad.

Secondly, I told the children, I don't want you to think that what happened to Jonathan was a punishment for his being bad. If you are remembering that Jonathan did something a little naughty a few days ago, and yesterday he was run over and died, it doesn't mean that if you sometimes do that same naughty thing, something bad is going to happen to you. Jonathan didn't get run over because he was a bad boy and deserved to get punished. He deserved to go on living, playing, and having fun, but this terrible, senseless accident happened.

Children who are upset by the sight of a crippled or handicapped person, or shy away from a blind person or a man with an artificial limb because they are frightened by the thought that something similar may happen to them, should be given a similar explanation: I don't know what happened to that man. Maybe he was in an accident. Maybe he had a serious disease. Maybe he was in the army, fighting to protect this country, and was wounded. It certainly doesn't mean that he was a bad person whom God is punishing. (Think of all the fairy tales in which hunchbacks, misshapen people, people with missing limbs, like Peter Pan's archfoe, Captain Hook, are portrayed as subhuman villains who threaten children.) We can try to urge young children to be aware of the ninety-five percent of a person that is normal, rather than the one organ that is flawed, in the people they see and in themselves. Sometimes, talking openly with a crippled or handicapped person about his artificial limb or missing vision can ease the barrier of strangeness and dispel the fear the child feels. (This won't always be possible though. Sometimes crippled or handicapped people find it hard to be stared at or to talk about their infirmities. For their own emotional stability, they may find it necessary to be taken as just like anyone else.)

Children are particularly susceptible to feelings of guilt. But even as adults, many of us never totally outgrow that tendency. A wrong word, even by someone trying to be helpful, will serve to reinforce the feeling that it was, in fact, our fault.

Beverly was crushed when her husband announced that he was leaving her. They had been married five years. They had no children; he had convinced her that they couldn't afford to have her leave her job quite yet. They had had arguments, but Beverly thought their marriage was no better and no worse than those of their friends. Then, one Saturday morning, he told her he had decided to leave. He said that he found her boring, that he was finding other women he had met more interesting, and that he did not think it was fair to either of them to be "stuck with each other" under the circumstances. An hour later, he had packed his clothes and was on his way to a friend's apartment. Stunned, Beverly drove to her parents' home and broke the news to them. They cried with her, comforted her, alternated between bitterness at her husband and practical advice about lawyers, house keys, and bank accounts.

After dinner that evening, Beverly's mother, a caring and concerned woman, took her aside and tried to talk to her about it. Trying to be helpful, she asked about their sex life, their finances, their patterns of interaction, looking for any clue to what might have caused the problem. Suddenly Beverly threw down her coffee cup and burst out, "Will you please stop this? I'm tired of hearing, 'Maybe if you had done this' and 'Maybe if you hadn't done that.' You make it sound like it was all my fault. You're telling me that if I had tried

101

harder to be a good wife, he wouldn't have left me. Well, that's not fair. I was a good wife. I don't deserve to have this happen. It's not my fault!"

And she was right, even as her mother was right to try to talk to her and comfort her. It is gratuitous, even cruel, to tell the person who has been hurt, whether by divorce or death or other disaster, "Maybe if you had acted differently, things would not have turned out so badly." When we say that, all we are really telling them is, "This is your fault for having chosen as you did." Sometimes marriages fail because people are immature, or because expectations are unrealistic on both sides. Sometimes people die because they have incurable diseases, not because their families turned to the wrong doctor or waited too long to go to the hospital. Sometimes businesses fail because economic conditions or powerful competition doom them, not because one person in charge made a wrong decision in a crucial moment. If we want to be able to pick up the pieces of our lives and go on living, we have to get over the irrational feeling that every misfortune is our fault, the direct result of our mistakes or misbehavior. We are really not that powerful. Not everything that happens in the world is our doing.

Some years ago, I officiated at the funeral of a thirty-eight-year-old woman who had died of leukemia, leaving a husband and one child, a boy of fifteen. As I entered the family's home after the burial, I heard an aunt say to the boy, "Don't feel bad, Barry. God took your mother because He needed her now more than you did." I give the aunt the benefit of the doubt: surely she was trying to make Barry feel better. She was trying somehow to make sense of a horrible and tragic event. But it seems to me that she did at least three things seriously wrong in those two sentences.

First of all, she told Barry not to feel bad. Yet why shouldn't he feel bad on the day of his mother's funeral? Why shouldn't he be entitled to honest feelings of pain, anger, loss? Why should he have to censor his honest, legitimate feelings in order to make the day easier for other people?

Second, she explained his mother's death in terms of God "taking her away." I don't believe that. It doesn't fit my understanding of God, and it can serve only to make Barry resentful of God and less open to the comforting ministrations of religion.

But most seriously of all, she suggested that God had taken Barry's mother "because He needed her now more than you did." I think I understand what she was trying to say. She wanted to say that her sister-in-law's death was not meaningless, that it served some purpose in God's scheme of things. But I suspect that was not the message that Barry got. What Barry heard was, "It's your fault that your mother died. You didn't need her enough. If you had needed her more, she would still be alive."

Can you remember what it was like to be fifteen years old, taking your first faltering steps toward independence, loving and needing your parents and yet impatient with the fact that you needed them, eager for the day when you could outgrow your need for them and be on your own? If Barry was a typical fifteen-year-old, he ate the food his parents bought and cooked for him, wore the clothes they purchased for him, lived in a room in their house, had to ask them to drive him where he needed to go, and dreamed of the day when he wouldn't need them in those ways any more. Then suddenly his mother died, and his aunt explained her death by saying, "You didn't need her enough, that's why she died." That was not what he needed to hear that day.

I had to spend many hours with Barry, overcoming his initial anger at me as the representative of the cruel God who had snatched his mother from him, overcoming his reluctance to discuss a painful subject which he was afraid would point up his guilt and shame. I had to persuade him that his mother's death was not his fault. She didn't die because he resented her, neglected her, aggravated her, or sometimes wished she would get out of his life. She died because she had leukemia. I told him I didn't know why his mother got leukemia. I didn't know why anybody gets it. But I believed as strongly as I believe anything that God had not willed it, not as a punishment for him, not as a punishment for her. I said to Barry, as I feel religious people should say to those who have been hurt by life, "This was not your fault. You are a good, decent person who deserves better. I can understand that you feel hurt, confused, angry at what happened, but there is no reason why you should feel guilty. As a man of faith, I have come here in God's name, not to judge you, but to help you. Will you let me help you?"

Whenever bad things happen to good people, there is likely to be the feeling that we might have prevented the misfortune if we had acted differently. And there will almost certainly be feelings of anger. It seems to be instinctive to become angry when we are hurt. I stub my toe against a chair, and I am angry at the chair for being there, and angry at myself for not watching where I was going. One of the important questions when we are hurt and angry is, what do we do with our anger?

Linda, a school guidance counselor, came home one afternoon and found that her apartment had been robbed. Her television set and tape deck were gone. Jewelry that had been given to her by her grandmother was missing. Clothes were strewn all around the apartment; her lingerie drawer was emptied onto the floor. Linda was even more hurt and upset by this invasion of her privacy than she was by the monetary loss. Feeling almost physically violated, she fell into a chair and cried at the unfairness of it all. A complicated mixture of emotions washed over her. She felt hurt, ashamed without knowing why, angry at herself for not making the apartment more secure, angry at her job for keeping her away from home and leaving the apartment accessible to burglars, and for making her come home so emotionally drained that she couldn't handle this additional insult. She felt angry at the superintendent of the building and at the policeman on the corner for not protecting her property better, angry at the city for being so full of criminals and junkies, angry at the world in general for being so unfair. She had been hurt, and she knew that she was deeply upset, but she was confused about where to direct her anger.

Sometimes we turn our anger upon the person responsible for hurting us: the supervisor who fired us, the wife who walked out on us, the driver who caused the accident. Sometimes, because our anger is more than we can contain, we find someone to blame, guilty or not, convincing ourselves that they could have and should have prevented the tragedy. I have had people tell me about the death ten years ago of a wife or child, and in the course of telling their story, they will become just as angry as they were ten years ago at the doctor who couldn't be reached or who missed a diagnosis.

Some of the worst instances of this are the trading of accusations by husband and wife after a child has died. "Why weren't you watching him more carefully?" "Why weren't you home so that I wouldn't have had my hands full with so many things all over the house?" "Maybe if you had fed him better. . . ." "If he hadn't gotten chilled on that stupid fishing trip. . . ." "My side of the family has always been healthy; it's your relatives who are disease-prone." A man and a woman who care about each other have been badly hurt. Because they were hurt, they are angry, and they direct their anger at the closest available target.

Similar, but not quite as tragic, is the man who loses his job and takes his anger out on his wife. She distracted him from concentrating on his job with problems at home, she demoralized him, didn't entertain the boss or the important customer properly.

Sometimes, if we can't find another person to dump our anger on, we turn it on ourselves. The textbook definition of depression is anger turned inward instead of being discharged outward. I suspect we have all known people who become depressed after a death, a divorce, a rejection or loss of a job. They stayed home, slept till noon, neglected their personal appearance, and spurned all efforts at friendship. This is depression, our anger at being hurt turned inward onto ourselves. If we blame ourselves, we want to hurt ourselves, to punish ourselves for what we messed up.

And sometimes we are angry at God. Because we were

brought up to believe that everything that happens is His will, we hold Him responsible for what happened, or at the very least for not having prevented it from happening. Religious people stop being religious, perhaps because they find the prayers and ceremonies no longer express their feelings ("what do I have to be thankful for?"), perhaps as a way of "getting even with God." Sometimes tragedy makes nonreligious people religious in an angry, defiant way. "I have to believe in God" one man told me, "so that I have someone to blame, someone to curse and shout at, when I think of what I've gone through."

In his novel *The Promise*, Chaim Potok tells the story of a boy who becomes mentally ill because he can't handle his anger at his father. Michael Gordon loves and admires his father so much that he can't face the fact that he often resents him and feels angry toward him. The psychiatrist, Danny Saunders, is able to help Michael because he has had to work through his own ambivalent feelings of love-hate-admiration-anger toward his own powerful, admirable, dominating father, and has done so successfully. One of the fascinating minor characters in *The Promise* is Rabbi Kalman, a teacher in the rabbinical seminary attended by Danny's best friend (who is the book's narrator). Rabbi Kalman is a survivor of the Holocaust. His wife and children died in the concentration camps. He is a rigidly Orthodox Jew who considers it a sin even to raise questions about God and why He does things the way He does. One must believe wholeheartedly, without doubts.

While Potok never makes the point explicitly, I understood the character of Rabbi Kalman to be intended to provide a parallel to Danny Saunders and Michael Gordon. Just as Michael became sick because he couldn't handle his anger at his father, Rabbi Kalman has become a tyrannical, unsympathetic person because he can't face up to his anger at his Father in Heaven. Rabbi Kalman permits no doubting, no questioning of God, because somewhere in the recesses of his mind he knows how furiously angry he is at God for the death of his family, and he knows that any questions will end in an angry outburst against God, maybe even the rejection of God and religion entirely. And he can't risk that happening. Is Rabbi Kalman afraid that his anger, should he ever unleash it, is so powerful it would destroy God? Or is he afraid that, should he ever reveal how angry he is, God will punish him even further?

In the novel, Michael is made whole by being taught not to be afraid of his anger. His anger is normal, understandable, and a lot less destructive than he has believed. He is told, to his immense relief, that it is all right to be angry at people you love. But no one tells Rabbi Kalman that it is all right to be angry at God.

Actually, being angry at God won't hurt God, and neither will it provoke Him to take measures against us. If it makes us feel better to vent our anger at Him over a painful situation, we are free to do it. The only thing wrong with doing it is that what happened to us was not really God's fault.

What do we do with our anger when we have been hurt? The goal, if we can achieve it, would be to *be angry at the situation*, rather than at ourselves, or at those who might have prevented it or are close to us trying to help us, or at God who let it happen. Getting angry at ourselves makes us depressed.

Being angry at other people scares them away and makes it harder for them to help us. Being angry at God erects a barrier between us and all the sustaining, comforting resources of religion that are there to help us at such times. But being angry at the situation, recognizing it as something rotten, unfair, and totally undeserved, shouting about it, denouncing it, crying over it, permits us to discharge the anger which is a part of being hurt, without making it harder for us to be helped.

Jealousy is almost as inevitable a part of being hurt by life as are guilt and anger. How can the injured person not feel jealous of people who may not deserve better, but have received better? How can the widow not be jealous of even her closest friends who still have a husband to go home to? How should the woman whose doctor has told her she will never be able to bear children react when her sister-in-law confides to her that something may have gone wrong and she may be pregnant a fourth time?

It serves no purpose to try to moralize against jealousy and talk people out of it. Jealousy is too strong a feeling. It touches us too deeply, hurting us in places we care about. Some psychologists trace the origins of jealousy to sibling rivalry. As children, we compete with our brothers and sisters for our parents' limited love and attention. It is so important to us, not only to be treated well, but to be treated better than the others. The white meat of the chicken, the largest dessert are not only servings of food but symbolic statements about which child our parents love most. It is that reassurance of winning the love contest, not the food, that we yearn for and compete for. (Did you know that the first mention of "sin" in the Bible is not in connection with Adam and Eve eating the forbidden fruit, but relates to Cain killing his brother Abel in a fit of jealousy, because God preferred Abel's offering to his own?) When we grow up, we may never entirely outgrow those childhood habits of competition, of needing to be reassured that we are "more loved," even as we may never totally outgrow the habit of thinking of God as a Heavenly Parent. For us to suffer an accident or bereavement is bad enough. But for us to suffer it while those around us don't is even worse, because that awakens all the old childhood competitiveness in us, and seems to proclaim to all that God loves them more than He loves us.

We can understand the logic of the statement that we would not be any healthier if our friends and neighbors were seriously ill, nor would we take any pleasure in their being sick. We can know full well that we would be just as lonely in our bereavement if our friends' husbands died, and we don't really want that to happen. (It will happen one day, and then we will have to contend with our guilt feelings for having wished it.) We can know all that, and still feel resentful toward them for having their health, their families, their jobs when we have lost ours. We can even understand that as we resent the good fortune of the people around us, we make it harder for them to help us, because they sense the resentment and the estrangement. We hurt ourselves more than anyone else by feeling jealous, and we know it. But we still feel it.

There is an old Chinese tale about the woman whose only son died. In her grief, she went to the holy man and said, "What prayers, what magical incantations do you have to bring my son back to life?" Instead of sending her away or reasoning with her, he said to her, "Fetch me a mustard seed from a home that has never known sorrow. We will use it to drive the sorrow out of your life." The woman set off at once in search of that magical mustard seed. She came first to a splendid mansion, knocked at the door, and said, "I am looking for a home that has never known sorrow. Is this such a place? It is very important to me." They told her, "You've certainly come to the wrong place," and began to describe all the tragic things that had recently befallen them. The woman said to herself, "Who is better able to help these poor unfortunate people than I, who have had misfortune of my own?" She stayed to comfort them, then went on in her search for a home that had never known sorrow. But wherever she turned, in hovels and in palaces, she found one tale after another of sadness and misfortune. Ultimately, she became so involved in ministering to other people's grief that she forgot about her quest for the magical mustard seed, never realizing that it had in fact driven the sorrow out of her life.

Perhaps that is the only cure for jealousy, to realize that the people we resent and envy for having what we lack, probably have wounds and scars of their own. They may even be envying us. The married woman who tries to comfort her widowed neighbor may have reason to fear that her husband will lose his job. She may have a delinquent child to worry about. The pregnant sister-in-law may have gotten some disturbing news about her own health. When I was a young rabbi, people would often resist my efforts to help them in their sorrow. Who was I, young, healthy, gainfully employed, to come in and mouth clichés about sharing their pain? Over the years, though, as they learned more about our son's illness and prognosis, the resistance melted. They accepted my consolations now, because they no longer had reason to resent my good fortune as contrasted with their bad luck. I was no longer God's more favored child. I was their brother in suffering, and they were able to let me help them.

But everyone is our brother or sister in suffering. No one comes to us from a home which has never known sorrow. They come to help us because they too know what it feels like to be hurt by life.

I don't think we should confront one another with our troubles. ("You think you've got problems? Let me tell you my problems, and you'll realize how well off you are.") That sort of competitiveness accomplishes nothing. It is as bad as the competitiveness that spawns sibling rivalry and jealousy in the first place. The afflicted person is not looking for an invitation to join the Suffering Olympics. But it would help if we remembered this: Anguish and heartbreak may not be distributed evenly throughout the world, but they are distributed very widely. Everyone gets his share. If we knew the facts, we would very rarely find someone whose life was to be envied.

7

GOD CAN'T DO EVERYTHING, BUT HE CAN DO SOME IMPORTANT THINGS

It is shortly before eleven o'clock one night when the telephone rings at my home. I find that telephones have a special, ominous way of ringing late at night, telling you even before you answer them that something bad is happening. I answer, and the voice at the other end identifies himself as someone I have never met, nor is he a member of my congregation. He tells me that his mother is in the hospital, and will undergo a serious operation the following morning. Would I please say a prayer for her recovery? I try to get more information, but the man is clearly upset and in a state of turmoil. I settle for writing down his mother's Hebrew name, assure him that the prayer will be offered, and wish him and his mother well. I hang up and I feel troubled, as I often do after such a conversation.

Praying for a person's health, for a favorable outcome of an operation, has implications that ought to disturb a thoughtful person. If prayer worked the way many people think it does, no one would ever die, because no prayer is ever offered more sincerely than the prayer for life, for health and recovery from illness, for ourselves and for those we love.

If we believe in God, but we do not hold God responsible for life's tragedies, if we believe that God wants justice and fairness but cannot always arrange for them, what are we doing when we pray to God for a favorable outcome to a crisis in our life?

Do I—and does the man who called me—really believe in a God who has the power to cure malignancies and influence the outcome of surgery, and will do that only if the right person recites the right words in the right language? And will God let a person die because a stranger, praying on her behalf, got some of the words wrong? Who among us could respect or worship a God whose implicit message was "I could have made your mother healthy again, but you didn't plead and grovel enough"?

And if we don't get what we prayed for, how do we keep from being either angry with God, or feeling that we have been judged and found wanting? How do we avoid feeling that God has let us down just when we needed Him most? And how do we avoid the equally undesirable alternative of feeling that God has disapproved of us?

Imagine the mind and heart of a blind or crippled child who has been raised on pious stories with happy endings, stories of people who prayed and were miraculously cured. Imagine that child praying with all the sincerity and innocence he can muster, that God make him whole, like other children. And now imagine his grief, his anger turned outward at God and at those who told him those stories, or turned inward on himself, when he realizes that his handicap is going to be permanent.

What better way to teach children to hate God than to teach them that God could have cured them, but "for their own good" chose not to?

There are several ways in which we can answer the person who asks, "Why didn't I get what I prayed for?" And most of the answers are problematic, leading to feelings of guilt, or anger, or hopelessness.

—You didn't get what you prayed for, because you didn't deserve it.
—You didn't get what you prayed for, because you didn't pray hard enough.
—You didn't get what you prayed for, because God knows what is best for you better than you do.
—You didn't get what you prayed for, because someone else's prayer for the opposite result was more worthy.
—You didn't get what you prayed for, because prayer is a sham; God doesn't hear prayers.
—You didn't get what you prayed for because there is no God.

If we are not satisfied with any of these answers, but don't want to give up on the idea of prayer, there is one other possibility. We can change our understanding of what it means to pray, and what it means for our prayers to be answered.

The Talmud, the compilation of discussions of Jewish Law which I have quoted earlier in this book, gives examples of bad prayers, improper prayers, which one should not utter. If a woman is pregnant, neither she nor her husband should pray, "May God grant that this child be a boy" (nor, for that matter, may they pray that it be a girl). The sex of the child is determined at conception, and God cannot be invoked to change it. Again, if a man sees a fire engine racing toward his neighborhood, he should not pray, "Please God, don't let the fire be in my house." Not only is it mean-spirited to pray that someone else's house burn instead of yours, but it is futile. A certain house is already on fire; the most sincere or articulate of prayers will not affect the question of which house it is.

We can extend this logic to contemporary situations. It would be equally improper for a high school senior, holding a letter from a college admissions office, to pray, "Please God, let it be an acceptance," or for a person waiting for the report of a biopsy to pray, "please God, let everything be all right." As with the Talmudic cases of the pregnant woman and the burning house, certain conditions already exist. We cannot ask God to go back and rewrite the past.

Neither, as we have suggested already, can we ask God to change laws of nature for our benefit, to make fatal conditions less fatal or to change the inexorable course of an illness. Sometimes miracles do happen. Malignancies mysteriously disappear; incurable patients recover, and baffled doctors credit it to an act of God. All we can do in a case like that is echo the doctor's bewildered gratitude. We don't know why some people spontaneously recover from illnesses which kill or cripple others. We don't know why some people die in car crashes or plane crashes, while other people, sitting right next to them, walk away with a few cuts and bruises and a bad scare. I can't believe that God chooses to hear the prayers of some and not of others. There would be no discernible rhyme or reason to His doing that. No amount of research into the lives of those who died and those who survived would help us learn how to live or how to pray so that we too would win God's favor.

When miracles occur, and people beat the odds against their survival, we would be well advised to bow our heads in thanks at the presence of a miracle, and not think that our prayers, contributions or abstentions are what did it. The next time we try, we may wonder why our prayers are ineffective.

Another category of prayer not fit for praying would be prayers meant to do someone else harm. If prayer, like religion as a whole, is meant to enlarge our souls, it should not be put to the service of meanness, envy, or vengeance. The story is told of two shopkeepers who were bitter rivals. Their stores were across the street from each other, and they would spend each day sitting in the doorway, keeping track of each other's business. If one got a customer, he would smile in triumph at his rival. One night, an angel appeared to one of the shopkeepers in a dream and said, "God has sent me to teach you a lesson. He will give you anything you ask for, but I want you to know that, whatever you get, your competitor across the street will get twice as much. Would you be wealthy? You can be very wealthy, but he will be twice as rich. Do you want to live a long and healthy life? You can, but his life will be longer and healthier. You can be famous, have children you will be proud of, whatever you desire. But whatever you get, he will get twice as much." The man frowned, thought for a moment, and said, "All right, my request is: strike me blind in one eye."

Finally, we cannot ask God in prayer to do something

which is within our power, so as to spare us the chore of doing it. A contemporary theologian has written these words:

> We cannot merely pray to You, O God, to end war;
> For we know that You have made the world in a way
> That man must find his own path to peace
> Within himself and with his neighbor.
> We cannot merely pray to You, O God, to end starvation;
> For you have already given us the resources
> With which to feed the entire world
> If we would only use them wisely.
> We cannot merely pray to You, O God,
> To root out prejudice,
> For You have already given us eyes
> With which to see the good in all men
> If we would only use them rightly.
> We cannot merely pray to You, O God, to end despair,
> For You have already given us the power
> To clear away slums and to give hope
> If we would only use our power justly.
> We cannot merely pray to You, O God, to end disease,
> For you have already given us great minds with which
> To search out cures and healing,
> If we would only use them constructively.
> Therefore we pray to You instead, O God,
> For strength, determination, and willpower,
> To do instead of just to pray,
> To become instead of merely to wish.
>
> JACK RIEMER,
> *Likrat Shabbat*

If we cannot pray for the impossible, or the unnatural, if we cannot pray out of a sense of revenge or irresponsibility, asking God to do our work for us, what is left for us to pray for? What can prayer do for us, to help us when we hurt?

The first thing prayer does for us is to put us in touch with other people, people who share the same concerns, values, dreams, and pains that we do. At the end of the nineteenth century and the beginning of the twentieth, one of the founders of the discipline of sociology was a Frenchman by the name of Emile Durkheim. The grandson of an Orthodox rabbi, Durkheim was interested in the role that society played in shaping a person's religious and ethical outlook. He spent years in the South Sea islands studying the religion of primitive natives in order to find out what religion was like before it was formalized with prayer books and professional clergy. In 1912, he published his important book *Elementary Forms of the Religious Life*, in which he suggested that the primary purpose of religion at its earliest level was not to put people in touch with God, but to put them in touch with one another. Religious rituals taught people how to share with their neighbors the experiences of birth and bereavement, of children marrying and parents dying. There were rituals for planting and for harvesting, for the winter solstice and for the vernal equinox. In that way, the community would be able to share the most joyous and the most frightening moments of life. No one would have to face them alone.

I think that is still what religion does best. Even people who are not ordinarily ritually inclined respond to a traditional wedding in the presence of friends and neighbors, with familiar words spoken and familiar ceremonies performed, even though their marriage would be just as legal if it were performed in the privacy of a judge's chambers. We need to share our joys with other people, and we need even more to share our fears and our grief. The Jewish custom of sitting *shiva*, the memorial week after a death, like the Christian wake or chapel visit, grows out of this need. When we feel so terribly alone, singled out by the hand of fate, when we are tempted to crawl off in a dark corner and feel sorry for ourselves, we need to be reminded that we are part of a community, that there are people around who care about us and that we are still part of the stream of life. At this point, religion structures what we do, forcing us to be with people and to let them into our lives.

So often, when I meet with a family after a death and before a funeral service, they will ask me, "Do we really need to sit *shiva*, to have all those people crowding into our living room? Couldn't we just ask them to leave us alone?" My response is, "No, letting people into your home, into your grief, is exactly what you need now. You need to share with them, to talk to them, to let them comfort you. You need to be reminded that you are still alive, and part of a world of life."

There is a marvelous custom in the Jewish mourning ritual called *se'udat havra'ah*, the meal of replenishment. On returning from the cemetery, the mourner is not supposed to take food for himself (or to serve others). Other people have to feed him, symbolizing the way the community rallies around him to sustain him and to try to fill the emptiness in his world.

And when the mourner attends services to recite the Mourners' Kaddish, the prayer recited for a year after a death, he feels the context of a supportive, sympathetic congregation around him. He sees and hears other mourners, bereaved even as he is, and he feels less singled out by adverse fate. He is comforted by their presence, by his being accepted and consoled by the community rather than being shunned as a victim whom God has seen fit to punish.

In the incident with which this chapter began, a stranger phoned me to ask me to pray for his mother, who was going to be operated on. Why did I agree, if I don't believe that my prayers (or his, for that matter) will move God to affect the results of the surgery? By agreeing, I was saying to him, "I hear your concern about your mother. I understand that you are worried and afraid of what might happen. I want you to know that I and your neighbors in this community share that concern. We are with you, even though we don't know you, because we can imagine ourselves being in your situation and wanting and needing all the support we can get. We are hoping and praying along with you that things turn out well, so that you don't have to feel that you are facing this frightening situation alone. If it helps you, if it helps your mother, to know that we too are concerned and hoping for her recovery, let me assure you that that is the case." And I firmly believe that knowing that people care *can* affect the course of a person's health.

Prayer, when it is offered in the right way, redeems people from isolation. It assures them that they need not feel alone and abandoned. It lets them know that they are part of a greater reality, with more depth, more hope, more courage, and more of a future than any individual could have by himself. One goes to a religious service, one recites the traditional prayers, not in order to find God (there are plenty of other places where He can be found), but to find a congregation, to find people with whom you can share that

121

which means the most to you. From that point of view, just being able to pray helps, whether your prayer changes the world outside you or not.

That wonderful storyteller Harry Golden makes this point in one of his stories. When he was young, he once asked his father, "If you don't believe in God, why do you go to synagogue so regularly?" His father answered, "Jews go to synagogue for all sorts of reasons. My friend Garfinkle, who is Orthodox, goes to talk to God. I go to talk to Garfinkle."

But that is only half of the answer to our question "what good does it do to pray?"—perhaps the less important half. Beyond putting us in touch with other people, prayer puts us in touch with God. I am not sure prayer puts us in touch with God the way many people think it does—that we approach God as a supplicant, a beggar asking for favors, or as a customer presenting Him with a shopping list and asking what it will cost. Prayer is not primarily a matter of asking God to change things. If we can come to understand what prayer can and should be, and rid ourselves of some unrealistic expectations, we will be better able to call on prayer, and on God, when we need them most.

Let me contrast two prayers found in the Bible, both spoken by the same person, in almost the same circumstances, twenty years apart. Both are found in the Book of Genesis, in the cycle of stories about the lives of the patriarchs.

In chapter 28, Jacob is a young man, spending his first night away from home. He has left his parents' home, having quarreled with his father and brother, and is traveling on foot to the land of Aram to live with his uncle Laban. Scared and inexperienced, feeling ashamed of what he has done at home and not knowing what lies in store for him at Laban's house, he prays, "If God will be with me on this venture, protecting me, giving me food to eat and clothes to wear, and if I come back safe to my father's house, then the Lord will be my only God. I will dedicate an altar to Him and set aside a tenth of all I earn for Him." Jacob's prayer here is the prayer of a frightened young man who is setting out to do something hard, is not sure he can do it, and thinks he can "bribe" God to make things work out for him. He is prepared to make it worth God's while to protect him and make him prosper, and he apparently believes in a God whose favor can be won and whose protection can be bought with promises of prayer, charity, and exclusive worship. His attitude, much like that of so many people today facing illness or misfortune, is expressed in this way: "Please God, make this work out well and I'll do whatever You want. I'll stop lying, I'll go to services regularly—You name it and I'll do it if You just grant me this." When we are not personally involved, we can recognize the immaturity of this attitude, and the immature picture of God at work here. It is not immoral to think that way, but it is inaccurate. That is not the way the world works. God's blessings are not for sale.

Ultimately, Jacob learns that lesson. As the biblical account of his life continues, Jacob spends twenty years at Laban's house. He marries Laban's two daughters and has many children. He works hard and accumulates the beginnings of a small fortune. Then the day comes for him to take his wives and children, his flocks and herds, and go home. He comes to the same river bank where he had stood and prayed in chapter 28. Again, he is anxious and afraid. Again, he is heading into a new country, an unfamiliar situation. He knows that the next day he will have to confront his brother Esau, who had threatened to kill him twenty years earlier. Once again, Jacob prays. But this time, because he is twenty years older and wiser, he offers a very different prayer than he did as a boy. In chapter 32 of Genesis, Jacob prays: "God of my father Abraham and of my father Isaac, I am unworthy of all the kindness You have shown me. I last crossed this river with nothing but my staff in my hand, and now I have grown to two camps. Deliver me, I pray, from my brother Esau, for I am afraid of him. . . . For it was You who said to me, I will make your offspring like the sand of the sea."

In other words, Jacob's prayer no longer tries to make a deal with God, nor does it present God with a long list of demands—food, clothing, prosperity, a safe return. It acknowledges that there is no currency in which God can be paid for blessing and helping us. Jacob's mature prayer says simply, "God, I have no claims on You and nothing to offer You. You have already given me more than I had any right to expect. There is only one reason for my turning to You now—because I need You. I am scared; I have to face up to something hard tomorrow, and I am not sure I can do it alone, without You. God, you once gave me reason to believe that I was capable of making something of my life. If You meant it, then You had better help me now, because I can't handle this alone."

Jacob doesn't ask God to make Esau go away, to cripple Esau's strength or magically erase his memory. Jacob asks God only to make him less afraid, by letting him know that He is at his side, so that whatever the next day might bring, he will be able to handle it because he won't have to face it alone.

That is the kind of prayer that God answers. We can't pray that He make our lives free of problems; this won't happen, and it is probably just as well. We can't ask Him to make us and those we love immune to disease, because He can't do that. We can't ask Him to weave a magic spell around us so that bad things will only happen to other people, and never to us. People who pray for miracles usually don't get miracles, any more than children who pray for bicycles, good grades, or boyfriends get them as a result of praying. But people who pray for courage, for strength to bear the unbearable, for the grace to remember what they have left instead of what they have lost, very often find their prayers answered. They discover that they have more strength, more courage than they ever knew themselves to have. Where did they get it? I would like to think that their prayers helped them find that strength. Their prayers helped them tap hidden reserves of faith and courage which were not available to them before. The widow who asks me on the day of her husband's funeral, "What do I have to live for now?", yet in the course of the ensuing weeks finds reasons to wake up in the morning and look forward to the day; the man who has lost his job or closed his business and says to me, "Rabbi, I'm too old and tired to start all over again," but starts over again nonetheless—where did they get the strength, the hope, the optimism that they did not have on the day they asked me those questions? I would like to believe that they received those things from the context of a concerned community, people who made it clear to them that they cared, and from the knowledge that God is at the side of the afflicted and the downcast.

If we think of life as a kind of Olympic games, some of life's crises are sprints. They require maximum emotional concentration for a short time. Then they are over, and life returns to normal. But other crises are distance events. They ask us to maintain our concentration over a much longer period of time, and that can be a lot harder.

I have visited people in the hospital after they have been badly burned or had their backs broken in accidents. For the first few days, they are grateful to be alive and full of confidence. "I'm a fighter; I'll beat this." In those first days, friends and family cluster around them, supportive and solicitous about their well-being, full of sympathy and concern. Then, as days grow into weeks and months, the pace of the extended crisis takes its toll on patient and relative alike. The sick person grows impatient with the sameness of the daily routine and the lack of discernible progress. He becomes angry at himself for not healing faster, or at the doctors for not having the magic to produce instant results. The wife who was so solicitous when her husband's lung cancer was diagnosed, finds herself becoming testy and impatient. "Sure, I feel sorry for him, but I'm a person with needs too. For years he overworked himself, neglected his health, and now that it has caught up with him, he expects me to give up my own life and become his nursemaid." Of course she loves her husband, and of course she feels terrible that he is so sick. But she may be getting tired of an ordeal with no end in sight. She may be afraid of being left a widow, concerned about her financial future, angry at him for getting sick (especially if he had in fact been smoking or neglecting his health), worn out from sleepless nights of worry. She is experiencing fear and fatigue, but it comes out as impatience and anger.

Similarly, the parents of a retarded child face a long-term situation with no prospect of a happy ending. The early years of sympathy, resignation, taking delight in every faltering step and garbled word, may give way to a time of frustration and anger as the child falls further behind his age-mates, and forgets even those things they have so painstakingly taught him. Then, in all likelihood, the parents will feel guilty and blame themselves for losing patience with a child whose limitations are no fault of his own.

Where do such parents get the strength they will need to go on day after day? For that matter, how does the man suffering from inoperable cancer, or the woman with Parkinson's disease, find the strength and sense of purpose to get up and face each new day, when there is no prospect of a happy ending?

I believe that God is the answer for these people as well, but not in the same way. I don't believe that God causes mental retardation in children, or chooses who should suffer from muscular dystrophy. The God I believe in does not send us the problem; He gives us the strength to cope with the problem.

Where do you get the strength to go on, when you have used up all of your own strength? Where do you turn for patience when you have run out of patience, when you have been more patient for more years than anyone should be asked to be, and the end is nowhere in sight? I believe that God gives us strength and patience and hope, renewing our spiritual resources when they run dry. How else do sick people manage to find more strength and more good humor over the course of prolonged illness than any one person could possibly have, unless God was constantly replenishing their souls? How else do widows find the courage to pick up the pieces of their lives and go out to face the world alone, when on the day of their husband's funeral, they did not have that courage? How else do the parents of a retarded or brain-damaged youngster wake up every morning and turn again to their responsibilities, unless they are able to lean on God when they grow weak?

We don't have to beg or bribe God to give us strength or hope or patience. We need only turn to Him, admit that we can't do this on our own, and understand that bravely bearing up under long-term illness is one of the most human, and one of the most godly, things we can ever do. One of the things that constantly reassures me that God is real, and not just an idea that religious leaders made up, is the fact that people who pray for strength, hope, and courage so often find resources of strength, hope, and courage that they did not have before they prayed.

I also believe that sick children should pray. They should pray for the strength to bear what they have to bear. They should pray that sickness and its treatment not hurt them too much. They should pray as a way of talking out their fears without the embarrassment of having to say them out loud, and as a reassurance that they are not alone. God is close to them even late at night in the hospital when their parents have gone home and all the doctors have left. God is still with them even when they are so sick that their friends no longer come to visit. The fear of pain and the fear of abandonment are perhaps the most troubling aspects of a child's illness, and prayer should be used to ease those fears. Sick children can even pray for a miracle to restore them to good health, as long as they do not feel that God is judging them to decide whether or not they deserve a miracle. They should pray because the alternative would be giving up all hope and marking time until the end comes.

"If God can't make my sickness go away, what good is He? Who needs Him?" God does not want you to be sick or crippled. He didn't make you have this problem, and He doesn't want you to go on having it, but He can't make it go away. That is something which is too hard even for God. What good is He, then? God makes people become doctors and nurses to try to make you feel better. God helps us be brave even when we're sick and frightened, and He reassures us that we don't have to face our fears and our pains alone.

The conventional explanation, that God sends us the burden because He knows that we are strong enough to handle it, has it all wrong. Fate, not God, sends us the problem. When we try to deal with it, we find out that we are not strong. We are weak; we get tired, we get angry, overwhelmed. We begin to wonder how we will ever make it through all the years. But when we reach the limits of our own strength and courage, something unexpected happens. We find reinforcement coming from a source outside of ourselves. And in the knowledge that we are not alone, that God is on our side, we manage to go on.

It was in this way that I answered the young widow who challenged me about the efficacy of prayer. Her husband had died of cancer, and she told me that while he was terminally ill, she prayed for his recovery. Her parents, her in-laws, and her neighbors all prayed. A Protestant neighbor invoked the prayer circle of her church, and a Catholic neighbor sought the intercession of St. Jude, patron saint of hopeless causes. Every variety, language, and idiom of prayer was mustered on his behalf, and none of them worked. He died right on schedule, leaving her and her young children bereft of a husband and father. After all that, she said to me, how can anyone be expected to take prayer seriously?

Is it really true, I asked her, that your prayers were not answered? Your husband died; there was no miraculous cure for his illness. But what did happen? Your friends and relatives prayed; Jews, Catholics, and Protestants prayed. At a time when you felt so desperately alone, you found out that you were not alone at all. You found out how many other people were hurting for you and with you, and that is no small thing. They were trying to tell you that this was not happening to you because you were a bad person. It was just a rotten, unfair thing that no one could help. They were trying to tell you that your husband's life meant a lot to them too, and not only to you and your children, and that whatever happened to him, you would not be totally alone. That is what their prayers were saying, and I suspect that it made a difference.

And what about *your* prayers?, I asked her. Were they left unanswered? You faced a situation that could easily have broken your spirit, a situation that could have left you a bitter, withdrawn woman, jealous of the intact families around you, incapable of responding to the promise of being alive. Somehow that did not happen. Somehow you found the strength not to let yourself be broken. You found the resiliency to go on living and caring about things. Like Jacob in the Bible, like every one of us at one time or another, you faced a scary situation, prayed for help, and found out that you were a lot stronger, and a lot better able to handle it, than you ever would have thought you were. In your desperation, you opened your heart in prayer, and what happened? You didn't get a miracle to avert a tragedy. But you discovered people around you, and God beside you, and strength within you to help you survive the tragedy. I offer that as an example of a prayer being answered.

～8

WHAT GOOD, THEN, IS RELIGION?

IN A sense, I have been writing this book for
fifteen years. From the day I heard the word
"progeria" and was told what it meant, I knew
that I would one day have to face Aaron's declining and dying.
And I knew that, after he died, I would feel the need to write
a book, sharing with others the story of how we managed to
go on believing in God and in the world after we had been
hurt. I didn't know what I would call the book, and I wasn't
totally sure what I would say. But I knew that the page after
the title page would carry a dedication to Aaron. I could visualize the dedication to him, and under it, in my mind's eye, I
could see the quotation from the Bible, the words of King David
after the death of his son: "Absalom, my son! Would that I had
died instead of you!"

Then one day, a year and a half after Aaron's death, I
realized that I was visualizing that page differently in my
imagination. Now instead of the passage in which David
wishes he were dead and his son alive, I saw in my mind's eye
the words of David after the death of an earlier child, the
passage that I have in fact used in part on the dedication page
of this book:

When David saw the servants whispering, he said to them, Is the child dead? And they said, He is dead. And David rose and washed and changed his clothing and asked that food be set before him, and he ate. The servants said to him, What is this that you are doing? You fasted and wept for the child when he was alive, and now that he is dead, you get up and eat! And David said: While the child was yet alive, I fasted and wept, for I said, Who knows whether the Lord will be gracious to me and the child will live. But now that he is dead, why should I fast? Can I bring him back again? I shall go to him; but he will not return to me. (II Samuel 12:19–23)

I knew then that the time had come for me to write my book. I had gone beyond self-pity to the point of facing and accepting my son's death. A book telling people how much I hurt would not do anyone any good. This had to be a book that would affirm life. It would have to say that no one ever promised us a life free from pain and disappointment. The most anyone promised us was that we would not be alone in our pain, and that we would be able to draw upon a source outside ourselves for the strength and courage we would need to survive life's tragedies and life's unfairness.

I am a more sensitive person, a more effective pastor, a more sympathetic counselor because of Aaron's life and death than I would ever have been without it. And I would give up all of those gains in a second if I could have my son back. If I could choose, I would forego all the spiritual growth and depth which has come my way because of our experiences, and be what I was fifteen years ago, an average rabbi, an indifferent counselor, helping some people and unable to help others, and the father of a bright, happy boy. But I cannot choose.

I believe in God. But I do not believe the same things about Him that I did years ago, when I was growing up or when I was a theological student. I recognize His limitations. He is limited in what He can do by laws of nature and by the evolution of human nature and human moral freedom. I no longer hold God responsible for illnesses, accidents, and natural disasters, because I realize that I gain little and I lose so much when I blame God for those things. I can worship a God who hates suffering but cannot eliminate it, more easily than I can worship a God who chooses to make children suffer and die, for whatever exalted reason. Some years ago, when the "death of God" theology was a fad, I remember seeing a bumper sticker that read "My God is not dead; sorry about yours." I guess my bumper sticker reads "My God is not cruel; sorry about yours."

God does not cause our misfortunes. Some are caused by bad luck, some are caused by bad people, and some are simply an inevitable consequence of our being human and being mortal, living in a world of inflexible natural laws. The painful things that happen to us are not punishments for our misbehavior, nor are they in any way part of some grand design on God's part. Because the tragedy is not God's will, we need not feel hurt or betrayed by God when tragedy strikes. We can turn to Him for help in overcoming it, precisely because we can tell ourselves that God is as outraged by it as we are.

"Does that mean that my suffering has no meaning?" That is the most significant challenge that can be offered to the

134

point of view I have been advocating in this book. We could bear nearly any pain or disappointment if we thought there was a reason behind it, a purpose to it. But even a lesser burden becomes too much for us if we feel it makes no sense. Patients in a veterans' hospital who have been seriously wounded in combat have an easier time adjusting to their injuries than do patients with exactly the same injury sustained while fooling around on a basketball court or a swimming pool, because they can tell themselves that their suffering at least was in a good cause. Parents who can convince themselves that there is some purpose somewhere served by their child's handicap can accept it better for the same reason.

Do you remember the biblical story, in chapter 32 of Exodus, about Moses, how, when he came down from Mount Sinai and saw the Israelites worshiping the golden calf, he threw down the tablets of the Ten Commandments so that they shattered? There is a Jewish legend that tells us that while Moses was climbing down the mountain with the two stone tablets on which God had written the Ten Commandments, he had no trouble carrying them although they were large, heavy slabs of stone and the path was steep. After all, though they were heavy, they had been inscribed by God and were precious to him. But when Moses came upon the people dancing around the golden calf, the legend goes, the words disappeared from the stone. They were just blank stones again. And now they became too heavy for him to hold on to.

We could bear any burden if we thought there was a meaning to what we were doing. Have I made it harder for people to accept their illnesses, their misfortunes, their family tragedies by telling them that they are not sent by God as part of some master plan of His?

Let me suggest that the bad things that happen to us in our lives do not have a meaning when they happen to us. They do not happen for any good reason which would cause us to accept them willingly. But we can give them a meaning. We can redeem these tragedies from senselessness by imposing meaning on them. The question we should be asking is not, "Why did this happen to me? What did I do to deserve this?" That is really an unanswerable, pointless question. A better question would be "Now that this has happened to me, what am I going to do about it?"

Martin Gray, a survivor of the Warsaw Ghetto and the Holocaust, writes of his life in a book called *For Those I Loved*. He tells how, after the Holocaust, he rebuilt his life, became successful, married, and raised a family. Life seemed good after the horrors of the concentration camp. Then one day, his wife and children were killed when a forest fire ravaged their home in the south of France. Gray was distraught, pushed almost to the breaking point by this added tragedy. People urged him to demand an inquiry into what caused the fire, but instead he chose to put his resources into a movement to protect nature from future fires. He explained that an inquiry, an investigation, would focus only on the past, on issues of pain and sorrow and blame. He wanted to focus on the future. An inquiry would set him against other people— "was someone negligent? whose fault was it?"—and being against other people, setting out to find a villain, accusing other people of being responsible for your misery, only makes a lonely person lonelier. Life, he concluded, has to be lived for something, not just against something.

We too need to get over the questions that focus on the past and on the pain—"why did this happen to me?"—and ask instead the question which opens doors to the future: "Now that this has happened, what shall I do about it?"

Let me once again cite Dorothee Soelle, the German theologian whom we quoted in chapter 5, asking whose side we thought God was on in the concentration camps, the murderers' side or the victims' side. Soelle, in her book *Suffering*, suggests that "the most important question we can ask about suffering is whom it serves. Does our suffering serve God or the devil, the cause of becoming alive or being morally paralyzed?" Not "where does the tragedy come from?" but "where does it lead?" is the issue on which Soelle would have us focus. In this context she speaks of "the devil's martyrs." What does she mean by that phrase? We are familiar with the idea that various religions honor the memories of martyrs for God, people who died in such a way as to bear witness to their faith. By remembering their faith in the face of death, our own faith is strengthened. Such people are God's martyrs.

But the forces of despair and disbelief have their martyrs too, people whose death weakens other people's faith in God and in His world. If the death of an elderly woman in Auschwitz or of a child in a hospital ward leaves us doubting God and less able to affirm the world's goodness, then that woman and that child become "the devil's martyrs," witnesses *against* God, against the meaningfulness of a moral life, rather than witnesses in favor. But (and this is Soelle's most

137

important point) it is not the circumstances of their death that makes them witnesses for or against God. It is *our reaction* to their death.

The facts of life and death are neutral. We, by our responses, give suffering either a positive or a negative meaning. Illnesses, accidents, human tragedies kill people. But they do not necessarily kill life or faith. If the death and suffering of someone we love makes us bitter, jealous, against all religion, and incapable of happiness, *we* turn the person who died into one of the "devil's martyrs." If suffering and death in someone close to us bring us to explore the limits of our capacity for strength and love and cheerfulness, if it leads us to discover sources of consolation we never knew before, then *we* make the person into a witness for the affirmation of life rather than its rejection.

This means, Soelle suggests, that there is one thing we can still do for those we loved and lost. We could not keep them alive. Perhaps we could not even significantly lessen their pain. But the one crucial thing we can do for them after their death is to let them be witnesses for God and for life, rather than, by our despair and loss of faith, making them "the devil's martyrs." The dead depend on us for their redemption and their immortality.

Soelle's words make it clear how we can act positively in the face of tragedy. But what about God's role? If God does not cause the bad things that happen to good people, and if He cannot prevent them, what good is He at all?

First of all, God has created a world in which many more good things than bad things happen. We find life's disasters upsetting not only because they are painful but because they are exceptional. Most people wake up on most days feeling good. Most illnesses are curable. Most airplanes take off and land safely. Most of the time, when we send our children out to play, they come home safely. The accident, the robbery, the inoperable tumor are life-shattering exceptions, but they are very rare exceptions. When you have been hurt by life, it may be hard to keep that in mind. When you are standing very close to a large object, all you can see is the object. Only by stepping back from it can you also see the rest of its setting around it. When we are stunned by some tragedy, we can only see and feel the tragedy. Only with time and distance can we see the tragedy in the context of a whole life and a whole world. In the Jewish tradition, the special prayer known as the Mourners' Kaddish is not about death, but about life, and it praises God for having created a basically good and livable world. By reciting that prayer, the mourner is reminded of all that is good and worth living for. There is a crucial difference between denying the tragedy, insisting that everything is for the best, and seeing the tragedy in the context of a whole life, keeping one's eye and mind on what has enriched you and not only on what you have lost.

How does God make a difference in our lives if He neither kills nor cures? God inspires people to help other people who have been hurt by life, and by helping them, they protect them from the danger of feeling alone, abandoned, or judged. God makes some people want to become doctors and nurses, to spend days and nights of self-sacrificing concern with an intensity for which no money can compensate, in the effort to sustain life and alleviate pain. God moves people to want to be medical researchers, to focus their intelligence and energy on the causes and possible cures for some of life's tragedies. When I was a boy, early summer was the most pleasant weather of the year in New York City, but it was a time of dread for young families because of the fear of a polio epidemic. But human beings used their God-given intelligence to eliminate that fear. Throughout human history, there have been plagues and epidemics that wiped out whole cities. People felt that they had to have six or eight children so that some at least would survive to adulthood. Human intelligence has come to understand more about the natural laws concerning sanitation, germs, immunization, antibiotics, and has succeeded in eliminating many of those scourges.

God, who neither causes nor prevents tragedies, helps by inspiring people to help. As a nineteenth-century Hasidic rabbi once put it, "human beings are God's language." God shows His opposition to cancer and birth defects, not by eliminating them or making them happen only to bad people (He can't do that), but by summoning forth friends and neighbors to ease the burden and to fill the emptiness. We were sustained in Aaron's illness by people who made a point of showing that they cared and understood: the man who made Aaron a scaled-down tennis racquet suitable to his size, and the woman who gave him a small handmade violin that was a family heirloom; the friend who got him a baseball autographed by the Red Sox, and the children who overlooked his appearance and physical limitations to play stickball with him in the backyard, and who wouldn't let him get away with anything special. People like that were "God's language," His way of telling our family that we were not alone, not cast off.

In the same way, I firmly believe that Aaron served God's purposes, not by being sick or strange-looking (there was no reason why God should have wanted that), but by facing up so bravely to his illness and to the problems caused by his appearance. I know that his friends and schoolmates were affected by his courage and by the way he managed to live a full life despite his limitations. And I know that people who knew our family were moved to handle the difficult times of their own lives with more hope and courage when they saw our example. I take these as instances of God moving people here on earth to help other people in need.

And finally, to the person who asks "what good is God? Who needs religion, if these things happen to good people and bad people alike?" I would say that God may not prevent the calamity, but He gives us the strength and the perseverance to overcome it. Where else do we get these qualities which we did not have before? The heart attack which slows down a forty-six-year-old businessman does not come from God, but the determination to change his life-style, to stop smoking, to care less about expanding his business and care more about spending time with his family, because his eyes have been opened to what is truly important to him—those things come from God. God does not stand for heart attacks; those are nature's responses to the body's being overstressed. But God does stand for self-discipline and for being part of a family.

The flood that devastates a town is not an "act of God," even if the insurance companies find it useful to call it that. But the efforts people make to save lives, risking their own lives for a person who might be a total stranger to them, and the determination to rebuild their community after the flood waters have receded, do qualify as acts of God.

When a person is dying of cancer, I do not hold God responsible for the cancer or for the pain he feels. They have other causes. But I have seen God give such people the strength to take each day as it comes, to be grateful for a day full of sunshine or one in which they are relatively free of pain.

When people who were never particularly strong become strong in the face of adversity, when people who tended to think only of themselves become unselfish and heroic in an emergency, I have to ask myself where they got these qualities which they would freely admit they did not have before. My answer is that this is one of the ways in which God helps us when we suffer beyond the limits of our own strength.

Life is not fair. The wrong people get sick and the wrong people get robbed and the wrong people get killed in wars and in accidents. Some people see life's unfairness and decide, "There is no God; the world is nothing but chaos." Others see the same unfairness and ask themselves, "Where do I get my sense of what is fair and what is unfair? Where do I get my sense of outrage and indignation, my instinctive response of sympathy when I read in the paper about a total stranger who has been hurt by life? Don't I get these things from God? Doesn't He plant in me a little bit of His own divine outrage at injustice and oppression, just as He did for the prophets of the Bible? Isn't my feeling of compassion for the afflicted just a reflection of the compassion He feels when He sees the suffering of His creatures?" Our responding to life's unfairness with sympathy and with righteous indignation, God's compassion and God's anger working through us, may be the surest proof of all of God's reality.

Religion alone can affirm the afflicted person's sense of self-worth. Science can describe what has happened to a person; only religion can call it a tragedy. Only the voice of religion, when it frees itself from the need to defend and justify God for all that happens, can say to the afflicted person, "You are a good person, and you deserve better. Let me come and sit with you so that you will know that you are not alone."

None of us can avoid the problem of why bad things happen to good people. Sooner or later, each of us finds himself playing one of the roles in the story of Job, whether as victim of tragedy, as a member of the family, or as a friend-comforter. The questions never change; the search for a satisfying answer continues.

In our generation, the gifted poet Archibald MacLeish has given us his version of the Job story in a modern setting. The first half of his poetic drama *J.B.* retells the familiar story. J.B., the Job-figure, is a successful businessman surrounded by an attractive, loving family. Then one by one, his children die. His business fails, his health fails. Finally, his whole city and much of the world are destroyed in a nuclear war.

Three friends come to "comfort" J.B., just as in the biblical story, and once again their words are more self-serving than comforting. In MacLeish's version, the first comforter is a Marxist who assures J.B. that none of his suffering is his fault. He just had the bad luck to be a member of the wrong economic class at the wrong time. He was a capitalist at the time of capitalism's decline. Had he lived the same life in another century, he would not have been punished. He is not suffering for any of his own sins. He just got in the way of the steamroller of historical necessity. J.B. is not comforted by this view. It takes his own personal tragedy too lightly, by seeing him only as a member of a certain class.

The second comforter is a psychiatrist. J.B. is not guilty, he tells him, because there is no such thing as guilt. Now that we understand what makes human beings tick, we know that we do not choose. We only think we choose. Really, we simply respond to instinct. We do not act; we are acted upon. Therefore we have no responsibility, and no guilt.

J.B. answers that such a solution, describing him as the passive victim of blind instincts, robs him of his humanity. "I'd rather suffer every unspeakable suffering God sends, knowing that it was . . . I that acted, I that chose, than wash my hands with yours in that defiling innocence."

The third and last comforter is a clergyman. When J.B. asks him for what sin he is being punished so harshly, he replies "Your sin is simple. You were born a man. What is your fault? Man's heart is evil. What you have done? Man's will is evil." J.B. is a sinner worthy of punishment not because of anything specific he has done, but because he is a human being, and human beings are inevitably imperfect and sinful. J.B. answers him, "Yours is the cruelest comfort of them all, making the Creator of the Universe the miscreator of mankind, a party to the crimes He punishes." J.B. cannot turn for help and comfort to a God who is described as making man imperfect and then punishing him for his imperfection.

Having rejected the explanations of the three comforters, J.B. turns to God Himself, and as in the Bible, God answers, overwhelming J.B. with His awesomeness, quoting lines directly from the biblical speech out of the whirlwind.

Up to this point, MacLeish has given us the biblical story of Job in a modern setting. His ending, however, is radically different. In the Bible, the story ends with God rewarding Job for having put up with so much suffering, and gives him new health, new wealth, and new children. In the play, there are no heavenly rewards in the closing scene. Instead, J.B. goes back to his wife, and they prepare to go on living together and building a new family. Their love, not God's generosity, will provide the new children to replace the ones who died.

J.B. forgives God and commits himself to going on living. His wife says to him, "You wanted justice, didn't you? There isn't any. . . . there is only love." The two narrators, representing the perspectives of God and Satan, are baffled. How could a person who has suffered so much in life want more life? "Who plays the hero, God or him? Is God to be forgiven?" "Isn't He? Job was innocent, you may remember." MacLeish's Job answers the problem of human suffering, not with theology or psychology, but by choosing to go on living and creating new life. He forgives God for not making a more just universe, and decides to take it as it is. He stops looking for justice, for fairness in the world, and looks for love instead.

In the play's moving last lines, Job's wife says:

> The candles in churches are out,
> The stars have gone out in the sky.

Blow on the coal of the heart
And we'll see by and by. . . .

The world is a cold, unfair place in which everything they held precious has been destroyed. But instead of giving up on this unfair world and life, instead of looking outward, to churches or to nature, for answers, they look inward to their own capacities for loving. "Blow on the coal of the heart" for what little light and warmth we will be able to muster to sustain us.

In *Dimensions of Job*, edited by Nahum N. Glatzer, MacLeish has written an essay explaining what he was trying to say in the ending of his Job-play. "Man depends on God for all things; God depends on man for one. Without Man's love, God does not exist as God, only as creator, and love is the one thing no one, not even God Himself, can command. It is a free gift, or it is nothing. And it is most itself, most free, when it is offered in spite of suffering, of injustice, and of death." We do not love God because He is perfect. We do not love Him because He protects us from all harm and keeps evil things from happening to us. We do not love Him because we are afraid of Him, or because He will hurt us if we turn our back on Him. We love Him because He is God, because He is the author of all the beauty and the order around us, the source of our strength and the hope and courage within us, and of other people's strength and hope and courage with which we are helped in our time of need. We love Him because He is the best part of ourselves and of our world. That is what it means to love. Love is not the admiration of perfection, but the acceptance of an imperfect person with all his imperfections, because loving and accepting him makes us better and stronger.

Is there an answer to the question of why bad things happen to good people? That depends on what we mean by "answer." If we mean "is there an explanation which will make sense of it all?"—why is there cancer in the world? Why did my father get cancer? Why did the plane crash? Why did my child die?—then there is probably no satisfying answer. We can offer learned explanations, but in the end, when we have covered all the squares on the game board and are feeling very proud of our cleverness, the pain and the anguish and the sense of unfairness will still be there.

But the word "answer" can mean "response" as well as "explanation," and in that sense, there may well be a satisfying answer to the tragedies in our lives. The response would be Job's response in MacLeish's version of the biblical story— to forgive the world for not being perfect, to forgive God for not making a better world, to reach out to the people around us, and to go on living despite it all.

In the final analysis, the question of why bad things happen to good people translates itself into some very different questions, no longer asking why something happened, but asking how we will respond, what we intend to do now that it has happened.

Are you capable of forgiving and accepting in love a world which has disappointed you by not being perfect, a world in which there is so much unfairness and cruelty, disease and crime, earthquake and accident? Can you forgive its imperfec-

147

tions and love it because it is capable of containing great beauty and goodness, and because it is the only world we have?

Are you capable of forgiving and loving the people around you, even if they have hurt you and let you down by not being perfect? Can you forgive them and love them, because there aren't any perfect people around, and because the penalty for not being able to love imperfect people is condemning oneself to loneliness?

Are you capable of forgiving and loving God even when you have found out that He is not perfect, even when He has let you down and disappointed you by permitting bad luck and sickness and cruelty in His world, and permitting some of those things to happen to you? Can you learn to love and forgive Him despite His limitations, as Job does, and as you once learned to forgive and love your parents even though they were not as wise, as strong, or as perfect as you needed them to be?

And if you can do these things, will you be able to recognize that the ability to forgive and the ability to love are the weapons God has given us to enable us to live fully, bravely, and meaningfully in this less-than-perfect world?

I think of Aaron and all that his life taught me, and I realize how much I have lost and how much I have gained. Yesterday seems less painful, and I am not afraid of tomorrow.

$\backsim$ Acknowledgments

THE process of transforming an idea into a book is a long and complicated one. In my efforts, I was helped by many people. Arthur H. Samuelson of Schocken Books was an immensely supportive editor. His enthusiasm, early and late, made it easier for me to keep on writing and rewriting, and his suggestions for changes were invariably helpful. The members of the two congregations I have served in Great Neck, N.Y. and Natick, Mass. listened to my sermons, brought me their problems, and shared Aaron's life and death with my family; they can rightfully claim a share in this book's formulation. While all the case studies in the book are drawn from my pastoral experience, all are combinations of people I have known, and no resemblance to any specific individual is intended. Several close friends read the manuscript in various stages, and I am grateful for their advice and suggestions. But more than anyone else, my wife Suzette and our daughter Ariel shared Aaron's life and loss more intimately than anyone else could. My memories are their memories, and I pray that my consolations are theirs as well.

Natick, Mass. 1981   Harold S. Kushner